Mometrix TEST PREPARATION

CLEP®

Introductory Business Law Exam Secrets Study Guide

Dear Future Exam Success Story

First of all, **THANK YOU** for purchasing Mometrix study materials!

Second, congratulations! You are one of the few determined test-takers who are committed to doing whatever it takes to excel on your exam. **You have come to the right place.** We developed these study materials with one goal in mind: to deliver you the information you need in a format that's concise and easy to use.

In addition to optimizing your guide for the content of the test, we've outlined our recommended steps for breaking down the preparation process into small, attainable goals so you can make sure you stay on track.

We've also analyzed the entire test-taking process, identifying the most common pitfalls and showing how you can overcome them and be ready for any curveball the test throws you.

Standardized testing is one of the biggest obstacles on your road to success, which only increases the importance of doing well in the high-pressure, high-stakes environment of test day. Your results on this test could have a significant impact on your future, and this guide provides the information and practical advice to help you achieve your full potential on test day.

Your success is our success

We would love to hear from you! If you would like to share the story of your exam success or if you have any questions or comments in regard to our products, please contact us at **800-673-8175** or **support@mometrix.com**.

Thanks again for your business and we wish you continued success!

Sincerely,
The Mometrix Test Preparation Team

Written and edited by the Mometrix Exam Secrets Test Prep Team
Printed in the United States of America

TABLE OF CONTENTS

Introduction

Thank you for purchasing this resource! You have made the choice to prepare yourself for a test that could have a huge impact on your future, and this guide is designed to help you be fully ready for test day. Obviously, it's important to have a solid understanding of the test material, but you also need to be prepared for the unique environment and stressors of the test, so that you can perform to the best of your abilities.

For this purpose, the first section that appears in this guide is the **Secret Keys**. We've devoted countless hours to meticulously researching what works and what doesn't, and we've boiled down our findings to the five most impactful steps you can take to improve your performance on the test. We start at the beginning with study planning and move through the preparation process, all the way to the testing strategies that will help you get the most out of what you know when you're finally sitting in front of the test.

We recommend that you start preparing for your test as far in advance as possible. However, if you've bought this guide as a last-minute study resource and only have a few days before your test, we recommend that you skip over the first two Secret Keys since they address a long-term study plan.

If you struggle with **test anxiety**, we strongly encourage you to check out our recommendations for how you can overcome it. Test anxiety is a formidable foe, but it can be beaten, and we want to make sure you have the tools you need to defeat it.

Secret Key #1 – Plan Big, Study Small

There's a lot riding on your performance. If you want to ace this test, you're going to need to keep your skills sharp and the material fresh in your mind. You need a plan that lets you review everything you need to know while still fitting in your schedule. We'll break this strategy down into three categories.

Information Organization

Start with the information you already have: the official test outline. From this, you can make a complete list of all the concepts you need to cover before the test. Organize these concepts into groups that can be studied together, and create a list of any related vocabulary you need to learn so you can brush up on any difficult terms. You'll want to keep this vocabulary list handy once you actually start studying since you may need to add to it along the way.

Time Management

Once you have your set of study concepts, decide how to spread them out over the time you have left before the test. Break your study plan into small, clear goals so you have a manageable task for each day and know exactly what you're doing. Then just focus on one small step at a time. When you manage your time this way, you don't need to spend hours at a time studying. Studying a small block of content for a short period each day helps you retain information better and avoid stressing over how much you have left to do. You can relax knowing that you have a plan to cover everything in time. In order for this strategy to be effective though, you have to start studying early and stick to your schedule. Avoid the exhaustion and futility that comes from last-minute cramming!

Study Environment

The environment you study in has a big impact on your learning. Studying in a coffee shop, while probably more enjoyable, is not likely to be as fruitful as studying in a quiet room. It's important to keep distractions to a minimum. You're only planning to study for a short block of time, so make the most of it. Don't pause to check your phone or get up to find a snack. It's also important to **avoid multitasking**. Research has consistently shown that multitasking will make your studying dramatically less effective. Your study area should also be comfortable and well-lit so you don't have the distraction of straining your eyes or sitting on an uncomfortable chair.

The time of day you study is also important. You want to be rested and alert. Don't wait until just before bedtime. Study when you'll be most likely to comprehend and remember. Even better, if you know what time of day your test will be, set that time aside for study. That way your brain will be used to working on that subject at that specific time and you'll have a better chance of recalling information.

Finally, it can be helpful to team up with others who are studying for the same test. Your actual studying should be done in as isolated an environment as possible, but the work of organizing the information and setting up the study plan can be divided up. In between study sessions, you can discuss with your teammates the concepts that you're all studying and quiz each other on the details. Just be sure that your teammates are as serious about the test as you are. If you find that your study time is being replaced with social time, you might need to find a new team.

Secret Key #2 – Make Your Studying Count

You're devoting a lot of time and effort to preparing for this test, so you want to be absolutely certain it will pay off. This means doing more than just reading the content and hoping you can remember it on test day. It's important to make every minute of study count. There are two main areas you can focus on to make your studying count.

Retention

It doesn't matter how much time you study if you can't remember the material. You need to make sure you are retaining the concepts. To check your retention of the information you're learning, try recalling it at later times with minimal prompting. Try carrying around flashcards and glance at one or two from time to time or ask a friend who's also studying for the test to quiz you.

To enhance your retention, look for ways to put the information into practice so that you can apply it rather than simply recalling it. If you're using the information in practical ways, it will be much easier to remember. Similarly, it helps to solidify a concept in your mind if you're not only reading it to yourself but also explaining it to someone else. Ask a friend to let you teach them about a concept you're a little shaky on (or speak aloud to an imaginary audience if necessary). As you try to summarize, define, give examples, and answer your friend's questions, you'll understand the concepts better and they will stay with you longer. Finally, step back for a big picture view and ask yourself how each piece of information fits with the whole subject. When you link the different concepts together and see them working together as a whole, it's easier to remember the individual components.

Finally, practice showing your work on any multi-step problems, even if you're just studying. Writing out each step you take to solve a problem will help solidify the process in your mind, and you'll be more likely to remember it during the test.

Modality

Modality simply refers to the means or method by which you study. Choosing a study modality that fits your own individual learning style is crucial. No two people learn best in exactly the same way, so it's important to know your strengths and use them to your advantage.

For example, if you learn best by visualization, focus on visualizing a concept in your mind and draw an image or a diagram. Try color-coding your notes, illustrating them, or creating symbols that will trigger your mind to recall a learned concept. If you learn best by hearing or discussing information, find a study partner who learns the same way or read aloud to yourself. Think about how to put the information in your own words. Imagine that you are giving a lecture on the topic and record yourself so you can listen to it later.

For any learning style, flashcards can be helpful. Organize the information so you can take advantage of spare moments to review. Underline key words or phrases. Use different colors for different categories. Mnemonic devices (such as creating a short list in which every item starts with the same letter) can also help with retention. Find what works best for you and use it to store the information in your mind most effectively and easily.

Secret Key #3 – Practice the Right Way

Your success on test day depends not only on how many hours you put into preparing, but also on whether you prepared the right way. It's good to check along the way to see if your studying is paying off. One of the most effective ways to do this is by taking practice tests to evaluate your progress. Practice tests are useful because they show exactly where you need to improve. Every time you take a practice test, pay special attention to these three groups of questions:

- The questions you got wrong
- The questions you had to guess on, even if you guessed right
- The questions you found difficult or slow to work through

This will show you exactly what your weak areas are, and where you need to devote more study time. Ask yourself why each of these questions gave you trouble. Was it because you didn't understand the material? Was it because you didn't remember the vocabulary? Do you need more repetitions on this type of question to build speed and confidence? Dig into those questions and figure out how you can strengthen your weak areas as you go back to review the material.

Additionally, many practice tests have a section explaining the answer choices. It can be tempting to read the explanation and think that you now have a good understanding of the concept. However, an explanation likely only covers part of the question's broader context. Even if the explanation makes perfect sense, **go back and investigate** every concept related to the question until you're positive you have a thorough understanding.

As you go along, keep in mind that the practice test is just that: practice. Memorizing these questions and answers will not be very helpful on the actual test because it is unlikely to have any of the same exact questions. If you only know the right answers to the sample questions, you won't be prepared for the real thing. **Study the concepts** until you understand them fully, and then you'll be able to answer any question that shows up on the test.

It's important to wait on the practice tests until you're ready. If you take a test on your first day of study, you may be overwhelmed by the amount of material covered and how much you need to learn. Work up to it gradually.

On test day, you'll need to be prepared for answering questions, managing your time, and using the test-taking strategies you've learned. It's a lot to balance, like a mental marathon that will have a big impact on your future. Like training for a marathon, you'll need to start slowly and work your way up. When test day arrives, you'll be ready.

Start with the strategies you've read in the first two Secret Keys—plan your course and study in the way that works best for you. If you have time, consider using multiple study resources to get different approaches to the same concepts. It can be helpful to see difficult concepts from more than one angle. Then find a good source for practice tests. Many times, the test website will suggest potential study resources or provide sample tests.

Practice Test Strategy

If you're able to find at least three practice tests, we recommend this strategy:

Untimed and Open-Book Practice

Take the first test with no time constraints and with your notes and study guide handy. Take your time and focus on applying the strategies you've learned.

Timed and Open-Book Practice

Take the second practice test open-book as well, but set a timer and practice pacing yourself to finish in time.

Timed and Closed-Book Practice

Take any other practice tests as if it were test day. Set a timer and put away your study materials. Sit at a table or desk in a quiet room, imagine yourself at the testing center, and answer questions as quickly and accurately as possible.

Keep repeating timed and closed-book tests on a regular basis until you run out of practice tests or it's time for the actual test. Your mind will be ready for the schedule and stress of test day, and you'll be able to focus on recalling the material you've learned.

Secret Key #4 – Pace Yourself

Once you're fully prepared for the material on the test, your biggest challenge on test day will be managing your time. Just knowing that the clock is ticking can make you panic even if you have plenty of time left. Work on pacing yourself so you can build confidence against the time constraints of the exam. Pacing is a difficult skill to master, especially in a high-pressure environment, so **practice is vital**.

Set time expectations for your pace based on how much time is available. For example, if a section has 60 questions and the time limit is 30 minutes, you know you have to average 30 seconds or less per question in order to answer them all. Although 30 seconds is the hard limit, set 25 seconds per question as your goal, so you reserve extra time to spend on harder questions. When you budget extra time for the harder questions, you no longer have any reason to stress when those questions take longer to answer.

Don't let this time expectation distract you from working through the test at a calm, steady pace, but keep it in mind so you don't spend too much time on any one question. Recognize that taking extra time on one question you don't understand may keep you from answering two that you do understand later in the test. If your time limit for a question is up and you're still not sure of the answer, mark it and move on, and come back to it later if the time and the test format allow. If the testing format doesn't allow you to return to earlier questions, just make an educated guess; then put it out of your mind and move on.

On the easier questions, be careful not to rush. It may seem wise to hurry through them so you have more time for the challenging ones, but it's not worth missing one if you know the concept and just didn't take the time to read the question fully. Work efficiently but make sure you understand the question and have looked at all of the answer choices, since more than one may seem right at first.

Even if you're paying attention to the time, you may find yourself a little behind at some point. You should speed up to get back on track, but do so wisely. Don't panic; just take a few seconds less on each question until you're caught up. Don't guess without thinking, but do look through the answer choices and eliminate any you know are wrong. If you can get down to two choices, it is often worthwhile to guess from those. Once you've chosen an answer, move on and don't dwell on any that you skipped or had to hurry through. If a question was taking too long, chances are it was one of the harder ones, so you weren't as likely to get it right anyway.

On the other hand, if you find yourself getting ahead of schedule, it may be beneficial to slow down a little. The more quickly you work, the more likely you are to make a careless mistake that will affect your score. You've budgeted time for each question, so don't be afraid to spend that time. Practice an efficient but careful pace to get the most out of the time you have.

Secret Key #5 – Have a Plan for Guessing

When you're taking the test, you may find yourself stuck on a question. Some of the answer choices seem better than others, but you don't see the one answer choice that is obviously correct. What do you do?

The scenario described above is very common, yet most test takers have not effectively prepared for it. Developing and practicing a plan for guessing may be one of the single most effective uses of your time as you get ready for the exam.

In developing your plan for guessing, there are three questions to address:

- When should you start the guessing process?
- How should you narrow down the choices?
- Which answer should you choose?

When to Start the Guessing Process

Unless your plan for guessing is to select C every time (which, despite its merits, is not what we recommend), you need to leave yourself enough time to apply your answer elimination strategies. Since you have a limited amount of time for each question, that means that if you're going to give yourself the best shot at guessing correctly, you have to decide quickly whether or not you will guess.

Of course, the best-case scenario is that you don't have to guess at all, so first, see if you can answer the question based on your knowledge of the subject and basic reasoning skills. Focus on the key words in the question and try to jog your memory of related topics. Give yourself a chance to bring the knowledge to mind, but once you realize that you don't have (or you can't access) the knowledge you need to answer the question, it's time to start the guessing process.

It's almost always better to start the guessing process too early than too late. It only takes a few seconds to remember something and answer the question from knowledge. Carefully eliminating wrong answer choices takes longer. Plus, going through the process of eliminating answer choices can actually help jog your memory.

Summary: Start the guessing process as soon as you decide that you can't answer the question based on your knowledge.

How to Narrow Down the Choices

The next chapter in this book (**Test-Taking Strategies**) includes a wide range of strategies for how to approach questions and how to look for answer choices to eliminate. You will definitely want to read those carefully, practice them, and figure out which ones work best for you. Here though, we're going to address a mindset rather than a particular strategy.

Your odds of guessing an answer correctly depend on how many options you are choosing from.

Number of options left	5	4	3	2	1
Odds of guessing correctly	20%	25%	33%	50%	100%

You can see from this chart just how valuable it is to be able to eliminate incorrect answers and make an educated guess, but there are two things that many test takers do that cause them to miss out on the benefits of guessing:

- Accidentally eliminating the correct answer
- Selecting an answer based on an impression

We'll look at the first one here, and the second one in the next section.

To avoid accidentally eliminating the correct answer, we recommend a thought exercise called **the $5 challenge**. In this challenge, you only eliminate an answer choice from contention if you are willing to bet $5 on it being wrong. Why $5? Five dollars is a small but not insignificant amount of money. It's an amount you could afford to lose but wouldn't want to throw away. And while losing $5 once might not hurt too much, doing it twenty times will set you back $100. In the same way, each small decision you make—eliminating a choice here, guessing on a question there—won't by itself impact your score very much, but when you put them all together, they can make a big difference. By holding each answer choice elimination decision to a higher standard, you can reduce the risk of accidentally eliminating the correct answer.

The $5 challenge can also be applied in a positive sense: If you are willing to bet $5 that an answer choice *is* correct, go ahead and mark it as correct.

Summary: Only eliminate an answer choice if you are willing to bet $5 that it is wrong.

Which Answer to Choose

You're taking the test. You've run into a hard question and decided you'll have to guess. You've eliminated all the answer choices you're willing to bet $5 on. Now you have to pick an answer. Why do we even need to talk about this? Why can't you just pick whichever one you feel like when the time comes?

The answer to these questions is that if you don't come into the test with a plan, you'll rely on your impression to select an answer choice, and if you do that, you risk falling into a trap. The test writers know that everyone who takes their test will be guessing on some of the questions, so they intentionally write wrong answer choices to seem plausible. You still have to pick an answer though, and if the wrong answer choices are designed to look right, how can you ever be sure that you're not falling for their trap? The best solution we've found to this dilemma is to take the decision out of your hands entirely. Here is the process we recommend:

Once you've eliminated any choices that you are confident (willing to bet $5) are wrong, select the first remaining choice as your answer.

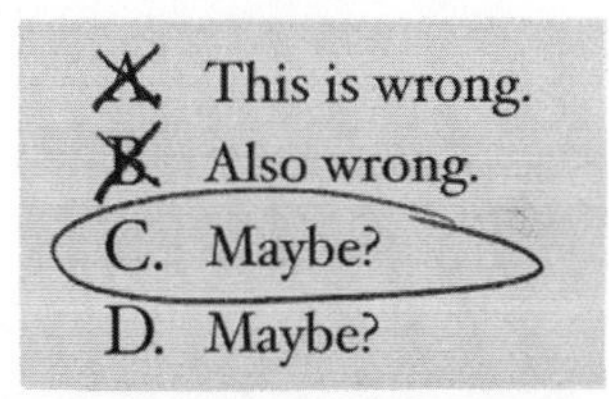

Whether you choose to select the first remaining choice, the second, or the last, the important thing is that you use some preselected standard. Using this approach guarantees that you will not be enticed into selecting an answer choice that looks right, because you are not basing your decision on how the answer choices look.

This is not meant to make you question your knowledge. Instead, it is to help you recognize the difference between your knowledge and your impressions. There's a huge difference between thinking an answer is right because of what you know, and thinking an answer is right because it looks or sounds like it should be right.

Summary: To ensure that your selection is appropriately random, make a predetermined selection from among all answer choices you have not eliminated.

Test-Taking Strategies

This section contains a list of test-taking strategies that you may find helpful as you work through the test. By taking what you know and applying logical thought, you can maximize your chances of answering any question correctly!

It is very important to realize that every question is different and every person is different: no single strategy will work on every question, and no single strategy will work for every person. That's why we've included all of them here, so you can try them out and determine which ones work best for different types of questions and which ones work best for you.

Question Strategies

☑ Read Carefully

Read the question and the answer choices carefully. Don't miss the question because you misread the terms. You have plenty of time to read each question thoroughly and make sure you understand what is being asked. Yet a happy medium must be attained, so don't waste too much time. You must read carefully and efficiently.

☑ Contextual Clues

Look for contextual clues. If the question includes a word you are not familiar with, look at the immediate context for some indication of what the word might mean. Contextual clues can often give you all the information you need to decipher the meaning of an unfamiliar word. Even if you can't determine the meaning, you may be able to narrow down the possibilities enough to make a solid guess at the answer to the question.

☑ Prefixes

If you're having trouble with a word in the question or answer choices, try dissecting it. Take advantage of every clue that the word might include. Prefixes can be a huge help. Usually, they allow you to determine a basic meaning. *Pre-* means before, *post-* means after, *pro-* is positive, *de-* is negative. From prefixes, you can get an idea of the general meaning of the word and try to put it into context.

☑ Hedge Words

Watch out for critical hedge words, such as *likely, may, can, often, almost, mostly, usually, generally, rarely*, and *sometimes*. Question writers insert these hedge phrases to cover every possibility. Often an answer choice will be wrong simply because it leaves no room for exception. Be on guard for answer choices that have definitive words such as *exactly* and *always*.

☑ Switchback Words

Stay alert for *switchbacks*. These are the words and phrases frequently used to alert you to shifts in thought. The most common switchback words are *but, although*, and *however*. Others include *nevertheless, on the other hand, even though, while, in spite of, despite*, and *regardless of*. Switchback words are important to catch because they can change the direction of the question or an answer choice.

✓ Face Value

When in doubt, use common sense. Accept the situation in the problem at face value. Don't read too much into it. These problems will not require you to make wild assumptions. If you have to go beyond creativity and warp time or space in order to have an answer choice fit the question, then you should move on and consider the other answer choices. These are normal problems rooted in reality. The applicable relationship or explanation may not be readily apparent, but it is there for you to figure out. Use your common sense to interpret anything that isn't clear.

Answer Choice Strategies

✓ Answer Selection

The most thorough way to pick an answer choice is to identify and eliminate wrong answers until only one is left, then confirm it is the correct answer. Sometimes an answer choice may immediately seem right, but be careful. The test writers will usually put more than one reasonable answer choice on each question, so take a second to read all of them and make sure that the other choices are not equally obvious. As long as you have time left, it is better to read every answer choice than to pick the first one that looks right without checking the others.

✓ Answer Choice Families

An answer choice family consists of two (in rare cases, three) answer choices that are very similar in construction and cannot all be true at the same time. If you see two answer choices that are direct opposites or parallels, one of them is usually the correct answer. For instance, if one answer choice says that quantity *x* increases and another either says that quantity *x* decreases (opposite) or says that quantity *y* increases (parallel), then those answer choices would fall into the same family. An answer choice that doesn't match the construction of the answer choice family is more likely to be incorrect. Most questions will not have answer choice families, but when they do appear, you should be prepared to recognize them.

✓ Eliminate Answers

Eliminate answer choices as soon as you realize they are wrong, but make sure you consider all possibilities. If you are eliminating answer choices and realize that the last one you are left with is also wrong, don't panic. Start over and consider each choice again. There may be something you missed the first time that you will realize on the second pass.

✓ Avoid Fact Traps

Don't be distracted by an answer choice that is factually true but doesn't answer the question. You are looking for the choice that answers the question. Stay focused on what the question is asking for so you don't accidentally pick an answer that is true but incorrect. Always go back to the question and make sure the answer choice you've selected actually answers the question and is not merely a true statement.

✓ Extreme Statements

In general, you should avoid answers that put forth extreme actions as standard practice or proclaim controversial ideas as established fact. An answer choice that states the "process should be used in certain situations, if..." is much more likely to be correct than one that states the "process should be discontinued completely." The first is a calm rational statement and doesn't even make a definitive, uncompromising stance, using a hedge word *if* to provide wiggle room, whereas the second choice is far more extreme.

⊘ Benchmark

As you read through the answer choices and you come across one that seems to answer the question well, mentally select that answer choice. This is not your final answer, but it's the one that will help you evaluate the other answer choices. The one that you selected is your benchmark or standard for judging each of the other answer choices. Every other answer choice must be compared to your benchmark. That choice is correct until proven otherwise by another answer choice beating it. If you find a better answer, then that one becomes your new benchmark. Once you've decided that no other choice answers the question as well as your benchmark, you have your final answer.

⊘ Predict the Answer

Before you even start looking at the answer choices, it is often best to try to predict the answer. When you come up with the answer on your own, it is easier to avoid distractions and traps because you will know exactly what to look for. The right answer choice is unlikely to be word-for-word what you came up with, but it should be a close match. Even if you are confident that you have the right answer, you should still take the time to read each option before moving on.

General Strategies

⊘ Tough Questions

If you are stumped on a problem or it appears too hard or too difficult, don't waste time. Move on! Remember though, if you can quickly check for obviously incorrect answer choices, your chances of guessing correctly are greatly improved. Before you completely give up, at least try to knock out a couple of possible answers. Eliminate what you can and then guess at the remaining answer choices before moving on.

⊘ Check Your Work

Since you will probably not know every term listed and the answer to every question, it is important that you get credit for the ones that you do know. Don't miss any questions through careless mistakes. If at all possible, try to take a second to look back over your answer selection and make sure you've selected the correct answer choice and haven't made a costly careless mistake (such as marking an answer choice that you didn't mean to mark). This quick double check should more than pay for itself in caught mistakes for the time it costs.

⊘ Pace Yourself

It's easy to be overwhelmed when you're looking at a page full of questions; your mind is confused and full of random thoughts, and the clock is ticking down faster than you would like. Calm down and maintain the pace that you have set for yourself. Especially as you get down to the last few minutes of the test, don't let the small numbers on the clock make you panic. As long as you are on track by monitoring your pace, you are guaranteed to have time for each question.

⊘ Don't Rush

It is very easy to make errors when you are in a hurry. Maintaining a fast pace in answering questions is pointless if it makes you miss questions that you would have gotten right otherwise. Test writers like to include distracting information and wrong answers that seem right. Taking a little extra time to avoid careless mistakes can make all the difference in your test score. Find a pace that allows you to be confident in the answers that you select.

⊘ KEEP MOVING

Panicking will not help you pass the test, so do your best to stay calm and keep moving. Taking deep breaths and going through the answer elimination steps you practiced can help to break through a stress barrier and keep your pace.

Final Notes

The combination of a solid foundation of content knowledge and the confidence that comes from practicing your plan for applying that knowledge is the key to maximizing your performance on test day. As your foundation of content knowledge is built up and strengthened, you'll find that the strategies included in this chapter become more and more effective in helping you quickly sift through the distractions and traps of the test to isolate the correct answer.

Now that you're preparing to move forward into the test content chapters of this book, be sure to keep your goal in mind. As you read, think about how you will be able to apply this information on the test. If you've already seen sample questions for the test and you have an idea of the question format and style, try to come up with questions of your own that you can answer based on what you're reading. This will give you valuable practice applying your knowledge in the same ways you can expect to on test day.

Good luck and good studying!

History and Sources of American Law

US Constitution

The US Constitution was drafted during the Constitutional Convention by delegates or representatives from 12 of the 13 original. James Madison, the fourth President of the United States, was also influential in the composition of the Constitution, as were Thomas Jefferson, Thomas Paine, and John Adams. The delegates began composing the Constitution in May of 1787, and it was ratified on June 21, 1788.

Articles of Confederation

The Articles of Confederation acted as the precursor to the US Constitution. The Articles of Confederation were written in 1781 to provide a means by which the federal government would control or govern the newly independent American colonies. The Articles of Confederation were designed to ensure that the federal government would have limited powers since the colonists were wary of a strong central government as a result of abuses by the English monarchy. However, the Articles of Confederation narrowed congressional power too much, preventing the federal government from collecting taxes, which resulted in Congress being unable to pay debts or maintain an army or navy. Other limitations, such as a lack of power over interstate commerce and a lack of means through which states would settle disputes, necessitated the revision of the Articles and ultimately led to the Constitution.

Replacement of the Articles of Confederation

The US Constitution corrected various problems inherent in the Articles of Confederation. While still limiting federal power and ensuring that powers were reserved to the states, the Constitution granted the federal government the power to tax the states, the power to establish a federal court system, and the right to pass laws affecting interstate commerce. The Constitution also altered the original rule in the Articles of Confederation that stipulated that each state or colony had only one vote, since this rule was unfair to those states with a larger population.

Constitution as Law

The US Constitution was written and signed by delegates from the 12 original states at the Constitutional Convention. The original 12 delegates who had composed the Constitution signed the document on September 17, 1787. In order to be passed, however, the Constitution then had to be ratified and approved by nine special state conventions. There was much opposition at the time to the passing of the Constitution and fierce debates raged between those who wanted the Constitution to be passed and the anti-federalists who were afraid that the Constitution vested too much power in the federal government. Rhode Island was the final state to ratify the Constitution on May 29, 1790.

Opposition by Anti-Federalists

Anti-federalists believed that the Revolutionary War had been fought on the principles of protecting local government. They believed that the Constitution created a government too similar to that of a centralized and all-powerful monarchy and that the Constitution would inhibit states' rights. The Anti-federalists were also concerned about using a new and then-untested form of government, as no previous countries had adopted a democracy in the form of enumerated powers such as described in the US Constitution. The Anti-Federalists also took issue with the absence of a Bill of Rights in the Constitution to protect the individual rights of people and states.

BILL OF RIGHTS

The Bill of Rights consists of the first ten amendments to the US Constitution. The Bill of Rights was written to provide a guarantee of individual and state powers and to place limits on what the federal and state governments could impose upon the people. The Bill of Rights was written in order to secure ratification of the US Constitution. Before the state committees ratified the US Constitution and it became law, the anti-federalists and many of the representatives from the original states believed that the Constitution should not be passed because it lacked a Bill of Rights. These first ten amendments were added in order to appease the federalists, protect the rights of the people from oppression that the citizens had fought a revolutionary war to escape, and to ensure that the Constitution would get the votes it needed to pass.

The first amendment protects the right to freedom of speech, freedom of the press, and freedom of religion. The second amendment protects the right to keep and bear arms and to organize a citizen militia. The third amendment places limitations and rules on the quartering of soldiers. The fourth amendment guarantees the right to be secure in your person and to be free from unreasonable search and seizure. The Fifth Amendment guarantees a person's right to due process of the law before being deprived of any rights and protects a person from being made to incriminate himself. The sixth amendment guarantees a right to a trial and the right to confront one's accuser. The seventh amendment protects the right to a trial by jury. The eighth amendment prohibits cruel and unusual punishment. The ninth amendment specifies that the enumeration of rights in the Constitution is not meant to deny any other rights retained by the people. The tenth amendment mandates that any powers not expressly granted to the federal government are reserved for the states.

ENUMERATED POWERS

When the US Constitution was passed, the states wished to limit the power of the federal government. As such, the Bill of Rights specified that "The powers not delegated to the United States by the Constitution, nor prohibited by it to the States, are reserved to the States respectively, or to the people." This means that unless the Constitution specifically gives the federal government the power and right to regulate a certain issue or pass legislation on that issue, the issue is left to the exclusive jurisdiction of the states. The states may then pass any laws they wish to regulate or govern that area, provided that the regulations do not conflict with any provisions contained within the Constitution.

CREATION OF A COURT SYSTEM

Article III of the United States Constitution addresses the creation of the judicial branch of the government. Article III mandates that "the judicial power of the United States shall be vested in one supreme Court and in such inferior Courts as the Congress may from time to time ordain and establish." This means that the Supreme Court of the United States is the only court that the Constitution mandates must exist. All other district courts and courts on the State level were created by the government on a voluntary basis.

FEDERAL COURT SYSTEM

Article III Section 2 of the US Constitution that created the Federal court system mandates that the judicial power of the federal government extends only to cases arising under the Constitution, laws made under the authority of the Federal court, cases affecting ambassadors or other public officials, controversies between a citizen and a state, controversies between states, or controversies between a US citizen and a citizen of a foreign state.

Court of limited jurisdiction: The federal court system created by the Constitution is limited in much the same way that the power of the federal government is limited. Powers not expressly granted to the federal court system are reserved for the state courts. Federal courts have subject matter jurisdiction- or the right to hear cases on a subject – only if the controversy arises out of the Constitution or another federal law, if the US is a party, if the states are having a dispute, or if diversity of jurisdiction exists because the two citizens having a dispute are from different states. Since state courts have the authority to hear all other cases, state courts are courts of general jurisdiction and federal courts are courts of limited jurisdiction.

US Supreme Court

Judicial Review

The Supreme Court affirmed that it has the power of judicial review in a 1798 case called *Calder v. Bull*. In this case, the state court had made a decision to hold a new trial about the contents of a will, overruling a decision made by an earlier trial court. A dispute existed regarding whether the state had violated the ex post facto rule in the Constitution which mandates that no state can impose a new law on actions that took place before that law was passed. The Supreme Court reviewed the law passed by the state legislature, thus establishing the concept of judicial review of legislation.

The Supreme Court argued in *Calder v. Bull* that judicial review of state legislation was appropriate in order to ensure that the rights vested in the Constitution were upheld. There were numerous arguments set forth in *Calder v. Bull* explaining why the Supreme Court had the right to review state legislation and strike it down if it was determined to be unconstitutional. The crux of the arguments can be explained in Justice Paterson's words: "if, then, a government, composed of Legislative, Executive and Judicial departments, were established, by a Constitution, which imposed no limits on the legislative power, the consequence would inevitably be, that whatever the legislative power chose to enact, would be lawfully enacted, and the judicial power could never interpose to pronounce it void." This essentially means that if there is no limit on the legislature by the court, the legislature would essentially have no accountability for failing to abide by the Constitution and could pass whatever law it wished.

In *Martin v. Hunters Lessee*, a state court ruled in favor of the confiscation of property based on a law passed during the American Revolution allowing for the confiscation of loyalists' property. The Virginia Supreme Court upheld the confiscation of the property. The US Supreme Court then reviewed the decision. The Virginia Supreme Court argued that the US Supreme Court did not have the legal right to review decisions made by a state court. The US Supreme Court reviewed Virginia's argument and determined that any question of federal law was within the Supreme Court's right to review and they acted as the ultimate authority on issues relating to the Constitution, even if the original case had been decided by a state court. Therefore, the Supreme Court was permitted under the law to review any case that implicated the Constitution on a state level. This ruling was passed in 1816.

US Congress

The US Congress consists of the Senate and the House of Representatives. There are two houses in Congress because of a compromise reached during the drafting of the US Constitution so that all delegates and states would ratify the Constitution. The delegates who were wary of a strong central government worried about having only senators to represent the interests of the people in their states. As a result, the House of Representatives was created to more closely reflect the will of the people. Senators are thus elected by a whole state, while representatives are elected by more narrow geographic regions. Members of the House of Representatives are elected every two years so that citizens can quickly vote someone out who is not representing their interests, while members of the Senate are elected every six years.

System of Checks and Balances

US Government

The system of checks and balances in the US government creates three branches of government: executive, legislative and judicial. The president forms the executive branch and has the power to veto bills passed by the legislative branch. The legislature consists of the Senate and the House of Representatives. The legislative branch has the right to pass laws provided its members gain the required majority to vote on the law. The judiciary or judicial branch consists of the Supreme Court and the other courts as created by Congress. The judicial branch has the right to review legislation passed by the executive and legislative branches for constitutionality.

US Constitution

After abuses perpetrated upon the colonies by British rule, the men who drafted the US Constitution were wary of a strong central government. As a result, the delegates who drafted the Constitution wished to impose limitations on the power of the government to ensure that the rights of the people were protected. By creating a tri-cameral government and vesting each of the three branches with the right and authority to review the actions and decisions of the other branches, the Constitution ensures that no one central authority or power who can unfairly inhibit the rights of the individual.

Common Law

Common law is a concept that dates back to the middle ages. Common law is law distinct from that passed by the legislature. Common law is judge-made law and is created when a judge hears a case and issues an opinion on that case. The opinion and the rule set forth by the judge becomes the law for all future cases and applies in all similar situations unless or until a higher court overrules the decision made by the judge or until the legislature passes a rule altering the law made by the judge.

Relationship to Legislation

Legislation is formal law passed in code books by the federal or a state legislature. These bills and laws cannot possibly address every possible situation or contingency and sometimes the bills must be interpreted by the courts when applied in a particular case. The court interpretation regarding legislation becomes a part of the law on that piece of legislation unless or until the legislature changes the rules. Thus, common law essentially fills gaps created or left by the legislature.

Sources of American Law

American law derives from legislation passed by state or federal legislatures, common law or case law made by judges, and the federal and state constitutions. All laws passed by the federal government must comply with the US Constitution which dictates the supreme law of the land. All laws passed by state governments must comply with both federal and state constitutions. Laws passed by legislative bodies must be passed according to a majority vote by the processes set forth in the laws that created the legislature.

American Legal Systems and Procedures

STARE DECISIS

Stare decisis is a shortened version of the Latin phrase *Stare decisis et non quieta movere*. This phrase means "to stand by decisions and not to disturb settled matters" and explains the concept of precedent in the legal environment. Once a court makes a ruling on a certain issue or sets forth a rule or law, that rule or law will be applied by all courts within the same jurisdiction that are at or below the level of the court that made the ruling. The ruling becomes precedent and is not disturbed or changed unless or until a higher court overrules it or the legislature passes a rule changing it.

Stare decisis is important because people need to be able to predict the way in which the law will view their actions and the way in which a court will decide decisions. Since legislation and statutory law cannot possibly cover every contingency, individuals need to turn to judge-made law or case law to determine the rules that will apply. As such, citizens need to be able to count on the court ruling the same way in future cases as it has in the past. Stare decisis ensures that the court will not change its mind and alter the way in which it decides a case. The principle of *stare decisis* also explains why common law exists- since people know that courts will rule the same way and apply the same rules, the rules made by the courts become law.

BINDING PRECEDENT

Binding precedent means that a specific legal rule or law passed by a court is binding and controls the way in which subsequent decisions must be made. Precedent or judicial decisions are binding on lower courts within the same jurisdiction. For example, if a California appeals court issues a ruling that sets forth a legal rule, that legal rule is binding on all appeals courts within California and on all lower courts. It is not binding on courts within any other state, however. Rulings made by the Supreme Court of the United States are binding on all states and courts within the US, since the Supreme Court is the final arbitrator and the highest court in the land.

PERSUASIVE AUTHORITY

Persuasive authority is legal cases or rulings that are not binding but that can be used to persuade the court to act in a certain way. For example, if a state court in California rules on an issue, that state court's ruling would not be binding in any state other than California. However, a person arguing a case in New York could point to that ruling in order to try to convince the New York court to address the issue in the same way, if the New York court has not already dealt with and ruled on the issue. The more states who have ruled in a certain way, the more persuasive those combined rulings will be in convincing other states to follow suit.

PRIMARY AND SECONDARY SOURCES

Primary sources are legally binding sources of law, such as statutes and case law. Primary sources can be cited in briefs, motions, and pleadings to a court and used to argue that the court should decide a case in a certain way. Secondary sources, on the other hand, are sources that can be used to conduct legal research but that have no legal weight and should not be cited in court. Law reviews and law journals are examples of secondary sources.

RESEARCHING A LEGAL ISSUE

The first step when researching a legal issue is to define the questions of law- the items being disputed. The researcher should then generate keywords based on those questions of law. The keywords can be used to identify relevant statutes, code, administrative opinions, constitutions, and case law that may apply on the given issue. The laws researched should be primary binding authority within the jurisdiction.

Researching Case Law

Much of the law in the United States is made by judges in the form of case law. This body of common law is thus binding and governs in many legal situations where there is no on-point constitutional provision or legislation to tell the court how to decide the case. It is essential to research case law in order to determine what rules of law exist in the field of common law that the court will apply when deciding the case.

Analogizing and Distinguishing

Analogizing is done when a case is on-point or close to on-point and when one wants the judge to decide in the same way as a given situation. In other words, analogizing involves selecting a case that states a given rule of law and drawing similarities and distinctions between the facts in that case and the facts in the present case so the judge will decide the present case in the same way. Distinguishing, on the other hand, is done when you do not want the court to decide a particular case in the same way that a previous case has been decided. In such cases, the purpose is to point out the differences between the previous case and the case at hand.

Overruled, Questioned, and Upheld

"Overruled" means that a decision by a court has been changed or overturned by a court at the same level of authority or at a higher authority. The original decision which has been overruled is no longer good law and cannot be cited or relied upon in legal arguments. "Questioned" means that an existing legal decision has been questioned in subsequent cases and some later judges have determined that the decision may not be based on sound legal principles. Laws that have been questioned are still good laws as they have not been overruled, but may not be as persuasive in making legal arguments. "Upheld" means that later courts have agreed with and affirmed the legal decision or rule in question. When a rule is upheld, that gives it greater weight in the eyes of the court.

Subject Matter Jurisdiction

Subject matter jurisdiction means that the court has a vested interest in the subject of a case and thus has the authority to decide the case. Within the US legal system, federal courts have a limited subject matter jurisdiction. Federal courts are viewed as having an interest only in the application of the Constitution or other federal laws. As such, federal courts do not have jurisdiction over cases arising out of state law except in certain situations where diversity jurisdiction exists (i.e. when two people from different states are having a dispute about $10,000 or more). State courts have general jurisdiction over all matters, such as disputes about property in the state, disputes about contracts in the state, and disputes about injuries that occurred in the state.

Personal Jurisdiction

Personal jurisdiction refers to the fact that a person must have enjoyed some benefit of the particular state in order to be subject to the rule of its court. For example, a person who has never set foot in the state of California cannot reasonably be called upon to come to a California court to respond to a lawsuit. To determine if personal jurisdiction exists, the court looks at the involved parties' level of contact with the state. Owning property in a state, for example, automatically subjects you to personal jurisdiction within that state for any matters relating to that property.

Diversity Jurisdiction

Diversity jurisdiction vests jurisdiction in the federal government over a subject that would normally be decided by a state court. It exists when two people from different states have a dispute, or when a person has a dispute with a resident alien or other non-citizen. Diversity jurisdiction is grounded on the premise that states will be partial to their own citizens over non-citizens. The federal court will decide the case using state law, but will do so on an impartial manner without prejudice for one state or the other. In order for diversity jurisdiction to exist, the controversy must be valued at $10,000 or more.

Forum Shopping

Forum shopping occurs when there are two or more potential courts where a case can be heard. For example, if both a federal and state court have subject matter and personal jurisdiction over a case, the case could be brought in either court. The plaintiff may thus choose which forum he believes will be best in light of his case and which forum will provide the most favorable outcome. The defendant also has the opportunity to engage in forum shopping as he can elect to have a case removed to federal court if it is brought in state court.

Actual Case or Controversy

The US Constitution states that courts must only render decisions when an actual case or controversy exists. In other words, a court cannot review a law for constitutionality and issue an opinion, legal rule, or ruling unless someone has sued on that particular subject. The person suing must have actually been harmed in some way that legal redress can correct and must have standing to sue. The court can then issue an opinion which becomes part of binding case law, or it can declare an offending piece of legislation unconstitutional and thus invalid.

Double Jeopardy

Double jeopardy is precluded by the US Constitution and means that a person cannot be tried twice for the same crime, nor sued twice arising out of the same event. For example, if a person was tried for killing his wife and the prosecutor lost, the prosecutor could not try the person again for that same murder. To determine if double jeopardy applies, the court looks at whether the series of events giving rise to the second lawsuit or criminal case is substantially the same as the first.

Criminal Law and Civil Law

Criminal law is a body of law that is enforced by an officer of the court. For example, only a prosecutor can bring a criminal case against a defendant, and the prosecutor doesn't necessarily always need the cooperation of the victim to do so. For a criminal conviction, a defendant can be deprived of life or liberty. Civil law, on the other hand, governs private interactions between people. A civil case can be brought by one person against another if the plaintiff has standing to sue. The penalties for a civil case are monetary. The standard for proving a criminal case is more stringent than for proving a civil case; a criminal case must be proven beyond a reasonable doubt while a civil case must usually be proven by a preponderance of the evidence.

Administrative Agency

An administrative agency is an authoritative body created by the legislature to enforce a particular piece of legislation. For example, the Equal Employment Opportunity Commission is an administrative agency created to enforce anti-discrimination laws while the Worker's Compensation Board is created in each state to enforce and oversee state worker's compensation programs. Agencies are created by the piece of legislation they are designed to enforce and obtain their power of enforcement through a grant of power by the legislature.

Administrative agencies help to enforce legislation that is too massive to be enforced by the court system and the legislature. For example, the Social Security Administration oversees how social security decisions are made and how funds are allocated because it would be too much for any single government entity or court system to cope with the management work and potential disputes associated with making social security payments. When an administrative agency has been vested with the authority over a given area of law, the opinions and decisions of that agency are binding, and most disputes must first go through the agency before a court of law will hear appeals on the issue.

ARBITRATION

Arbitration is a form of alternative dispute resolution. Many contracts contain stipulations requiring parties to submit to binding arbitration. In such cases, an arbitration procedure is set forth by which an independent arbitrator hears the facts of a case and makes a legally binding decision. Courts will enforce both arbitration clauses and the decisions of arbitrators unless procedural unfairness is involved in the contract or arbitration process. Disputes settled by arbitration thus do not get settled in court.

ADVANTAGES AND DISADVANTAGES

For the court system, there are several advantages of arbitration. First, arbitration can be less expensive than a full trial with a judge and/or jury. Second, courts are not backlogged by as many cases when some cases are handled by arbitrators. Third, in highly specific or technical issues an arbitrator can be hired that has familiarity with that issue. There are also some disadvantages of arbitration. First, arbitration opinions do not add to the body of case law so there are fewer judicial decisions on certain commonly arbitrated issues. Second, there may always be some procedural bias in favor of the "repeat player" or the person or company who is more likely to arbitrate again. For example, if a private citizen is involved in a dispute against his insurance company, the arbitrator knows that the insurance company is likely to be a repeat customer while the private citizen is not. Thus the arbitrator may be subconsciously or consciously biased towards the insurance company.

Contracts

Sales of Goods Scenarios

Battle of Forms

A purchaser places an order with a seller for 100 items. One of the order's conditions states, "Purchaser may reject any defective goods within 30 days of receipt." The seller's letter of confirmation states, "Any objection to goods delivered must occur within 15 days of receipt." Twenty days after the purchaser receives the goods, he seeks to object to 25 of the items as being defective. This issue exemplifies the "battle of forms" question. If the purchaser had objected to the seller's 15-day stipulation, he should have notified the seller of this objection before completing the transaction. The purchaser's failure to object to the clause results in the seller's 15-day stipulation constituting part of the contract, to which the purchaser cannot object.

Sales of Stolen Goods

A concert violinist takes his car to a mechanic for a tune-up. The violinist inadvertently leaves his Stradivarius violin on the back seat. The mechanic sells the Stradivarius to a punk rocker. The concert violinist cannot recover the Stradivarius from the punk rocker, who is a bona fide purchaser in possession of the Stradivarius with a voidable title. The concert violinist can, however, sue the mechanic for the value of the Stradivarius.

Agreements Entered into Under Duress

An employer discovers that his employee has embezzled a sum of money while working at the employer's place of business. The employer agrees to not report the embezzlement if the employee will sign a 5-year promissory note. Agreements entered into under duress are judged to be illegal and invalid. Since the employer's promise to not report the embezzlement in exchange for the proffered note constitutes duress the employee can rescind the obligation.

Contracts

A contract is a legally enforceable agreement, whether express or implied, between two parties. A contract, though arising from a mutually voluntary agreement between parties, is entitled to the same enforcement as a law that society will enforce. Once the parties have made and entered into a contract, the contract is just as binding on the parties as a law, and neither party may violate the terms of the contract without the consent the other party. Note that a written document in and of itself does not constitute the totality of a contract, as a document only represents the mental condition that gave rise to the contract.

The four essential elements of a valid contract are:

- Capacity of the parties -- i.e., the parties must have the legal capacity to enter into the contract. Contracts involving minors or persons lacking sufficient mental capacity are voidable.
- Mutual agreement -- The buyer and the seller must agree on all terms of a contract.
- Consideration -- One party to a contract must give something of value in the common sense in exchange for a promise made by the other party.
- Legality -- The contract must not violate any jurisdictional laws.

Intent of Parties

Intent of the parties to a contract may be determined from the totality of the words and actions of the parties, in contrast to the parties' isolated words or actions. Contradictions and uncertainties may be resolved by employing common sense rules. Clear, bold print will be considered more significant than fine print or obscurely-placed print. Handwritten inter-lineation (i.e., writing between the lines) on a printed document provides strong evidence of intent. The conduct of the parties to a contract may override formal documents if that conduct clearly demonstrates an intent contrary to that which may be inferred from the documents.

UCC and Contracts for Merchants

The five principal ways the UCC (Uniform Commercial Code) changes sales contracts for merchants are:

- Higher standards of conduct must exist, namely good faith and reasonable commercial standards.
- Written confirmation of an oral agreement may satisfy the Statute of Frauds.
- A firm offer to purchase or to sell goods is irrevocable for up to three months.
- Even if an acceptance alters the terms of an offer, this does not necessarily constitute a rejection.
- The UCC provides for implied warranties of merchantability and ownership.

Types of Contracts

Five types of contracts are described below:

- Express contract -- a contract in which all elements (e.g., offer, acceptance, consideration) are specifically stated, whether in words, written or oral, or partly written and partly oral
- Implied-in-fact contract -- a contract in which the existence and terms are agreed to nonverbally, that is, by conduct
- Implied-in-law contract -- a contract created to avoid the unjust enrichment of one party at the expense of another, wherein the wronged party is entitled to receive restitution
- Bilateral contract -- a contract consisting of an exchange of promises between the parties
- Unilateral contract -- a contract consisting of a promise by one party and an act by the other party

Legal Offers and Acceptance of Offers

For an offer to be legally valid, it must adhere to the following requirements:

- The offer must indicate a clear intent to enter into a contract.
- The offer must be expressed with sufficient specificity so that that a court can ascertain the actual intent of the parties.
- The offer must be communicated to the party to whom the offer is made.

For acceptance of an offer to be considered valid, the acceptance must be clear and unconditional -- conditional acceptance is treated as a counter-offer, constituting a rejection. In the case of a unilateral offer, although commencement of the promised act by the offeror may be held to constitute acceptance, confirmation by the receiver will bind the offer as a bilateral contract. Silence only constitutes acceptance under certain conditions, for example if the parties mutually agree that silence means acceptance.

Consideration of Contracts

In the context of a contract, consideration is anything of commonly agreed upon worth that is promised to another when making a contract. Consideration may take the form of money, property, services or even the abstinence from some future action. A promise by one of the parties to perform some act that that party is already bound to perform, or the act of carrying out what is a moral duty, does not constitute consideration, however. Courts generally do not attempt to evaluate whether an exchange between parties is monetarily fair, but rather are concerned with the actual presence of consideration itself (an exception being the exchange of a small amount of money for a larger amount). Past consideration has no legal value: In a case where one party performed some act not expecting anything in return from another party and the second party subsequently promises some compensation for the benefit received, the second party's promise would not be legally valid.

Consideration may be deemed to be absent under the following conditions:

- Illusory promises -- When the promisor merely promises to do something if he wishes or needs to do so, the promise is not considered an actual one.
- Moral obligation -- To merely agree to do something that one would ordinarily be expected to do does not constitute consideration.
- Doing what one is bound to do -- Agreeing to perform an act that is within the scope of one's preexisting duties does not constitute consideration.
- Promissory estoppel -- In an agreement, although there may not otherwise be an enforceable contract, where it would be unfair not to enforce the agreement because one party has relied on the promise of the other.

Sales Contract Concepts Addressed by the UCC

The concepts of statute of frauds, greater flexibility than under common law, and interpretation of the agreement as addressed by the UCC are explained below:

- Statute of frauds -- Under the UCC, agreements for the sale of goods for $500 or more is covered by the statute of frauds.
- Greater flexibility than under common law -- Whereas under common law it is a requirement that the parties agree on a price, under UCC a contract need not necessarily specify a price. Rather, it is sufficient if the parties agree on a "reasonable" at the time the goods are delivered.
- Interpretation of the agreement -- The UCC specifies certain criteria by which to identify the intent of the parties in entering into a sales contract. These criteria address such considerations as performance, past conduct, and custom, as opposed to more technical considerations.

CISG

The CISG ratified by 75 nations, including the most important trading nations, governs law for most international sales transactions entered into by US companies. The CISG only applies to contracts between companies located in two different countries. (The companies are free to agree that other laws, not the CISG, will apply, however.) Items under the purview of the CISG include: (a) the CISG's "firm offer rule," which addresses under what conditions a contract cannot be revoked; (b) the CISG's "mirror image rule," which addresses discrepancies between an offer and its acceptance, which may constitute material alterations of the contract and thus its lack of validity.

Mirror Image Rule

The mirror image rule concerns contracts in which there is a material difference between an offer and its acceptance as it relates to price, payment, quality, and quantity of the goods in question, and including questions about such matters as the time and place of delivery, liability, and the manner in which disputes are to be settled. In essence, the mirror image rule negates the formation of a contract within which such material differences are present. Should the offeror of the goods receive a contrary response from the receiver and, failing to recognize the significance of the receiver's alteration, proceed as if the contract had been formed, the offeror may be considered to have accepted the receiver's alteration to the contract. Further, if the receiver's response to an offer contains material additions or limitations to it, then his response constitutes a rejection of the offer.

Obtaining a Better Title than the Seller

The three circumstances under which a buyer may obtain a better title than the seller has had are:

1. A party with a voidable title (a title that is subject to cancellation by the seller) can transfer a valid title to a bona fide purchaser (one who is unaware of the voidable title).
2. In cases involving the dealing of goods, a purchaser who purchases goods in good faith from a retailer will get a good title, even though the retailer in the ordinary course of his business has transferred to another party a prior interest in those goods.
3. In cases involving the dealing of goods, if a purchaser in good faith buys goods that have been entrusted to a retailer by a third party for some special purpose, the purchaser obtains good title to the goods he has purchased.

Destination Contract

What is meant by a destination contract and how the following create destination contracts:

- FOB (Free on Board) destination
- Ex-ship
- No arrival, no sale

A destination contract relates to the delivery of goods, in which the risk of loss is passed to the buyer upon delivery of the purchased goods to the destination specified in the contract. Destination contracts are created they following ways:

- FOB destination -- Free on board is a shipping term that indicates that the shipper pays the shipping costs to the specified destination. Upon the goods' arrival, the buyer takes responsibility.
- Ex-ship -- A seller is required to deliver goods to a buyer at an agreed port of arrival. The seller remains responsible for the goods until they are delivered, after which the buyer pays for the unloading and subsequent charges.
- No arrival, no sale -- In the case that the goods do not arrive, there is no contract. Neither seller nor buyer is responsible to the other, unless the seller is responsible for the non-arrival. The seller remains liable for goods arriving damaged or in violation of the contract.

SHIPMENT CONTRACT

A shipment contract is one under which the buyer assumes the risk of loss upon the seller's delivery of the goods to the carrier. The following are descriptions of acronyms for shipment contracts:

- FOB -- free on board. A term of sale whereby the seller's price includes all the charges incurred up to the point of placing the goods on board a ship at the specified point of departure.
- FAS -- free alongside ship. A term of sale whereby the seller's price includes the charges incurred only up to the ship at the specified point of departure. The buyer is responsible for all subsequent charges.
- CIF -- cost, insurance and freight. A term of sale whereby the seller's price includes insurance and all other charges up to the specified destination point.
- C & F -- cost and freight. A term of sale whereby the seller's price does not include insurance, but includes all expenses up to the specified destination point.

RISK OF LOSS

The risk of loss is determined thus under the following circumstances:

- When it is difficult or impossible to ascertain whether the contract is a shipment or a destination contract: If the seller is a merchant, he bears the risk of loss up to the point when the goods are delivered to the buyer. If the seller is not a merchant, the buyer bears the risk of loss when the goods become available to him.
- When the delivery of goods is performed by a person other than the seller or buyer: Unless the contract specifies otherwise, the buyer assumes the risk of loss upon receiving the documents of title.
- When there is a breach: If the goods are nonconforming and unaccepted, the seller retains or is assigned the risk. If the goods are conforming, the buyer who breaches the contract is liable for any uninsured loss or damage.

PERFORMANCE OBLIGATIONS

Article 2 Part 5 of the Uniform Commercial Code governs the performance of sales contracts. Unless specific provisions of the code deal specifically with the performance obligations of a particular sales contract, questions of performance are determined by the language of the contract itself or by the general law of contracts. In the absence of language in the sales contract to the contrary, the seller has an obligation to tender the goods, and the buyer has an obligation to tender payment. Typically, the obligation to make the first move falls upon the seller. The buyer has the right to inspect the goods before accepting or paying for them, whether in cash or by check, but is expected to tender payment before taking possession.

PERFECT TENDER RULE

The common law of contracts includes language indicating that performance of a sales contract is considered fulfilled if the performance is substantial. The "perfect tender rule," however, changes this common law with respect to the performance of the seller. Namely, the rule states that if the seller's performance fails in any respect to conform to the terms of the contract, then this substandard performance constitutes nonconformity with the contract. In the event a seller fails to conform to the perfect tender rule, the buyer has any one of the following means of recourse:

- He may reject all of the goods.
- He may accept all of the goods.
- He may accept only the conforming goods and reject the remaining, nonconforming, goods.

Conditions

Conditions may be defined as events whose occurrence or nonoccurrence alter, create, preclude or terminate a contract. The following types of conditions may be described thus:

- Express conditions -- deliberately created, agreed-upon conditions of a contract
- Implied conditions -- contained within most contracts, whether implied by law or by the language of the contract
- Time of performance -- typically a type of express (i.e., not implied) condition identifying performance of a contractual obligation at an expected time
- Satisfactory performance -- can be subjective (i.e., judged as a matter of personal preference) or objective (i.e., provable based upon observable standards)

Discharge of contracts

Discharge may be defined as the termination or completion of a contract. The following types of discharge may be described thus:

- Discharge by performance -- When the essential parts of a contract have been performed by both the buyer and the seller, the contract is considered discharged by performance.
- Discharge by breach -- When one party fails to perform in a substantial way, the contract is considered discharged by breach. Upon a breach by one party, the other party is no longer obliged to perform.
- Discharge by agreement of the parties -- By either mutual rescission, where both parties agree to terminate the contract, or by accord and satisfaction, where the parties agree to alter the terms of an existing obligation, is a contract discharged by agreement of the parties.

The four conditions under which a contract may be discharged by operation of law are:

- Subsequent illegality -- refers to the situation whereby a statute is enacted subsequent to the creation of a contract, which makes the contract newly illegal
- Impossibility -- occurring as a result of the death of one of the parties, the destruction of the property identified in the contract, or a law or government act that makes performance illegal
- Bankruptcy -- Upon a successful petition for bankruptcy, the debtor is released from all contractual obligations.
- Statute of limitations -- generally three to six years, depending on state law; (Note that if the promise to perform is renewed after the statute of limitations has expired, the contractual obligation is renewed.)

BFP for value

A bona fide purchaser (BFP) for value is an innocent party who in good faith attains from another party apparent legal title to the other party's property, in the absence of knowledge of any third party's claim to the title of that property. The bona fide purchaser must purchase the property or value, meaning that he must pay for it rather than merely receive it as a gift. A bona fide purchaser for value normally is not subject to liability for prior claims or liens on the property he purchases. Depending on the laws of the jurisdiction, even in the case of the seller fraudulently conveying the property to the bona fide purchaser as when the seller has already transferred the property to someone else, the bona fide purchaser will take good title to the property, assuming he has properly recorded the transaction in accordance with legal requirements.

Note that the third party to such a transaction retains the right to bring suit against the party that made the fraudulent conveyance.

NEGLIGENT ENTRUSTMENT

Negligent entrustment describes a situation in which one party (the entrustor) is held liable for negligence because he provided another party (the entrustee) with the means to cause injury to a third party. Negligent entrustment is most often applied in cases involving motor vehicles, but also commonly occurs in cases involving firearms or other such items with the potential to create harm. A key element in cases involving negligent entrustment is that the entrustee is known through reputation or through documentation to have the proclivity to use the specified instrument in a manner that is likely to cause harm.

EXPRESS WARRANTY

The term express warranty, in the context of sales contracts, refers to a spoken or written assurance by the seller concerning the nature, performance, or quality of the goods he is selling. The three kinds of representations that express a promise of warranty are:

1. An affirmation of the fact of conformance -- a statement asserting that the goods or services being sold will accomplish a specific purpose
2. A description of the goods -- this description constitutes a warranty that the delivered goods will conform to the manner in which they have been described or specified
3. Reference to a sample or model -- visual representations of the goods or services being sold (e.g., pictures, diagrams, drawings, or prototypes) serve as a warranty of the nature of the goods or services being sold

IMPLIED WARRANTY

The term implied warranty as it is used in the context of sales contracts arises specifically out of the buyer/seller relationship. An implied warranty is present in all sales transactions, arising from a common sense understanding of the relationship between the seller and buyer. An implied warranty has the same legal effect as an express warranty. The two kinds of representations that imply a promise of warranty are:

1. Warranty of merchantability -- a warranty imposed on the merchant, assuring that the goods he is selling are "fit for the ordinary purposes for which such goods are used"
2. Warranty of fitness -- a warranty imposed on any seller of goods or services, requiring that the seller possess knowledge and expertise on which the buyer may rely

DISCLAIMERS

A disclaimer in regards to the context of contracts for the sale of goods is a mechanism whereby the seller seeks to eliminate or modify legal warranty obligations, whether express or implied. Phrases such as "as is," "with all faults," or "without warranty" constitute the simplest and most direct type of disclaimer, with "as is" being particularly applicable in the sale of second-hand goods. For a disclaimer to be effective and likely to be looked upon favorably by the courts, the seller is obliged to make every effort to call attention to the disclaimer, by such means as bold type, such that it will be noticeable even to an uneducated or careless reader.

MAGNUSON-MOSS WARRANTY ACT

The Magnuson-Moss Warranty Act, passed by Congress in 1975, federally governs consumer product warranties. Affecting the rights of consumers and the obligations of warrantors in written warranties, the act requires manufacturers and sellers of consumer products to provide consumers with detailed information about warranty coverage. The three basic tenets of the act are:

1. A warrantor must specify his warranty as being either "full" or "limited."
2. A warranty must be part of an easy-to-read document, in which specified information relating to the scope of the coverage is delineated in simple, clear language.
3. A warrantor must ensure that the terms of his warranty are readily available for inspection by prospective buyers.

PRIVITY

Privity may be defined as the requirement that a party bringing a lawsuit on a contract be a party to the contract. The concept of privity as it relates to the process of recovery for breach of warranty takes two distinct forms:

1. From the point of view of the seller -- Can a seller be held liable for a breach of a product liability warranty in the case of injury to someone other than the purchaser himself? The courts generally rule in the affirmative if the seller could reasonably anticipate that such third parties might be injured by the product.
2. From the point of view of the buyer -- Here the question becomes: Can the buyer seek redress from someone else in the chain of distribution (e.g., a manufacturer or a distributor) with whom the buyer had no contact? As above, courts will generally rule in favor of the buyer if those more remote parties could have reasonably foreseen the potential for injury to the eventual buyer.

NEGLIGENT HARMFUL ACTION AND STRICT LIABILITY

As they relate to product liability arising from tort, the following concepts may be elaborated upon thus:

- Negligent harmful action -- Negligence exists in cases in which generally accepted standards of care are not followed and in which harm must have been reasonably foreseeable. Under the principle of res ipsa loquitur ("the thing speaks for itself"), (a) a plaintiff's injury would not ordinarily occur unless someone has been negligent; (b) a plaintiff's injury must result from a condition within the exclusive control of the defendant; and (c) the plaintiff must not have done anything that significantly contributed to the accident that caused the injury.
- Strict liability -- imposes liability on manufacturers and sellers even if they were not at fault or negligent, so long as (a) the product was defective at the time of its sale; (b) the seller's business concerns the selling of the product in question; and (c) the product when purchased differed in no substantive way from the product as produced.

PARTIES HELD LIABLE FOR DEFECTIVE PRODUCTS

The following parties in the chain of distribution may be held liable for a defective product under these conditions:

- Manufacturers -- may be liable for a defective product, even if it is the responsibility of a subsequent party (e.g., a distributor) to inspect and/or to correct defects
- Component part manufacturers -- not generally responsible for defects in a product's design, but are liable if a defect in their specific component's manufacture or design is the basis for the suit

- Wholesalers -- usually liable for defective products they sell, unless such defects are not ordinarily detectable
- Retailers -- often held liable, except in the case of some jurisdictions that may limit retailers' liability in cases in which they were in no way responsible for the defect

Defenses for Sellers in Product Liability Lawsuits

Defenses available to sellers that if proven may bar or limit a plaintiff's ability to recover damages in a product liability lawsuit include:

- Product misuse -- The plaintiff has used the product in a blatantly improper manner or has failed to properly maintain the product.
- Assumption of risk -- The product that the plaintiff has purchased has known risks or well-publicized side effects.
- Sophisticated purchaser -- applies in cases in which the plaintiff has specific knowledge or training as to render him extraordinarily knowledgeable about the product in question
- Preemption -- arises when federal statutes override state courts' jurisdiction to decide claims in the case in question
- State of the art -- The defendant utilized the best available technology available at the time, or the defendant exercised a high standard of care and could not have foreseen the danger inherent in the product at the time of manufacture.

Breach of Contract

Plaintiff's Case

The three essential elements of a plaintiff's case in a breach of contract action are:

1. The contract must be proven to exist.
2. Proof must exist that the defendant breached the contract.
3. Proof must exist that the breach by the defendant resulted in injury or damage to the plaintiff.

De Minimus

Courts employ the concept of de minimus (short for de minimus non curat lex -- "the law does not concern itself with trifles") in awarding damages in cases in which the damage to the plaintiff is so small as to be considered insignificant. In such cases, the court may award nominal damages ($1) or some other token amount. The intent of de minimus is to discourage plaintiffs from bringing cases to avenge some perceived embarrassment or hurt feelings.

Certainty, Foreseeability, Mitigation

As they relate to the ability to be legally compensated for damages in a breach of contract lawsuit, the following concepts may be described thus:

- Certainty -- Damages cannot be merely speculative, but must be proved to a reasonable certainty.
- Foreseeability -- A defendant cannot be held liable for damages that were not reasonably foreseeable (a) at the time the contract was created; or (b) at the time the contract was breached.
- Mitigation -- Compensatory damages are limited by the plaintiff's requirement to make reasonable efforts to minimize his loss. Failure to do so may result in a partial or complete inability to be compensated for a breach by the defendant.

Types of Damages Awarded

The following types of damages that may be awarded in a breach of contract lawsuit may be described thus:

- Consequential damages -- damages resulting not as a result of an act, but rather from a consequence of the act; the tests of certainty and foreseeability apply in full, and consequential damages can only be awarded if the breaching party knew or had reason to know that losses would result from the breach.
- Liquidated damages -- Since questions regarding the amount of damages can be complex, parties to a contract are strongly advised to include clauses specifying liquidated damages (i.e., dollar amounts). When liquidated damages are deemed to reflect reasonable efforts by the parties to calculate damages, such liquidated damages will be enforced by the court.
- Punitive damages -- Also termed exemplary damages, punitive damages are awarded as a punishment and example to deter others from malicious, evil or particularly fraudulent acts. Burden of proof is on the plaintiff, who must prove that the defendant's conduct was malicious, or in reckless disregard of the plaintiff's rights.

"Make Whole" Principle

The "make whole" principle of the Uniform Commercial Code may be applied to determine compensation for a party who has sustained a loss in a sales contract, whether the breach has been committed by either the buyer or the seller. The code states that the remedies for breach shall "be liberally administered to the end that the aggrieved party shall be put in as good a position as if the other party had fully performed..." In other words, the court is compelled to make every effort to award damages sufficient to restore the aggrieved party to the position in which he would have been without the fault of the other. The precise definition of the make whole principle varies, according to contract terms and local laws, and may include either actual economic losses or a combination of actual economic and non-economic losses, and not necessarily to the settlement value of the case. There is a four-year statute of limitations for a sales contract, within which a suit for breach must be filed.

Buyers in Breach of Sales Contracts

The four circumstances in which a buyer may be deemed in breach of a sales contract are:

- The seller proffers the goods, but the buyer refuses to accept them.
- After having received the goods, the buyer improperly returns them.
- After having received the goods, the buyer fails to pay for them.
- At any point during the proper execution of the contract, the buyer exhibits an unwillingness to go forward.

Among the remedies available to the seller in the event of a buyer's breach are:

- The seller may cancel the contract and delay delivery of the goods.
- The seller may resell the goods to another buyer and recover damages for the difference in price received (if any).
- The seller may seek to recover damages from the buyer.

Note that the aggrieved seller is not limited to choosing one option to the exclusion of the others.

Breach of Contract Categories

The following categories of breach of contract may be described thus:

- Minor breach -- also a partial breach or an immaterial breach; refers to the case in which the non-breaching party is only entitled to collect the actual amount of damages, but is not entitled to an order for performance of obligations
- Material breach -- a failure to perform that permits the non-breaching party to either compel performance or collect damages
- Fundamental breach -- in addition to entitling the non-breaching party to damages, permits this party to terminate performance of the contract
- Anticipatory breach -- occurs when one party to a contract reneges on his obligations under the contract, the result being that the other party is relieved of his obligations to perform under the contract. The idea is that one party cannot renounce his obligation and yet expect the other party to perform.

Defenses

The following possible defenses to breach of contract lawsuits may be described thus:

- Duress -- occurs when one or more of the parties to a contract are pressured, coerced, or forced into entering into a contract, thus negating their exercise of free will
- Unconscionable contract terms -- Unconscionability may be used as a legitimate defense to a breach of contract lawsuit if it is determined that the terms of the contract are unjust, unfair or outrageous.
- Unilateral or mutual mistakes -- when one party to a contract is mistaken as to the terms of the contract (unilateral) or both parties are so mistaken (mutual); this may constitute a legitimate defense for not performing as per the terms of the contract
- Impossibility of performance -- occurs when a party to a contract is unable, due to circumstances beyond his control (e.g., mental incapacity, death), to perform his contractual obligations

Document of Title

A document of title is any written instrument, such as a bill of sale, an order for the delivery of goods, or a warehouse receipt, that confers and/or proves that the person who possesses it is entitled to the goods to which the instrument refers. A document of title is typically issued by an individual who is in possession of another person's goods (the bailee) to the person who has entrusted to him the goods (the bailor). In addition to describing the goods in such a manner as to render them identifiable, the document of title must set forth the terms of the contractual agreement between the bailor and the bailee.

Negotiable and Non-Negotiable

A document of title is considered negotiable only if the document states that the goods referred to will be delivered to the bearer or to the order of any party identified in the title document. That is, negotiation of a document of title occurs by the person possessing the document merely endorsing the goods to the recipient, without having to physically move the goods.

A document of title is considered non-negotiable if it is not in such a form that it can be negotiated by delivery. The endorsement of a non-negotiable document of title gives the transferee no additional right, and a document of title is also considered non-negotiable if at the time of issue it contains a conspicuous legend stating that it is non-negotiable.

NEGOTIABLE INSTRUMENT

A negotiable instrument is a type of commercial paper that is defined as a document of title or evidence of indebtedness, which is unconditionally transferable in trading as a substitute for money. The three main attributes of a negotiable instrument are:

1. A transferor passes that asset or property that is the subject of the instrument to a transferee by delivery and/or by endorsement.
2. In accepting the instrument in good faith, the transferee immediately obtains non-forfeitable title, including his ability to file suit on that instrument in his name.
3. The party liable in the instrument does not need to be given any notice of the transfer.

The following are three types of negotiable instruments:

1. A note -- a two-party negotiable instrument, most often referred to as a promissory note, in which the maker proffers an unconditional promise in writing to pay the payee or the payee's designee a specific amount of money on demand or at a specified date
2. A draft -- a three-party negotiable instrument, in which the drawer orders the drawee to pay the payee a fixed amount of money on demand or at a specified date
3. A check -- a type of draft that is narrowly defined to reflect that the drawee is always a bank and the instrument is payable on demand

ADVANTAGES OVER ORDINARY CONTRACTS

Negotiable instruments are frequently preferred over ordinary contracts because negotiable instruments are usually easier to enforce. The rights of someone merely holding an ordinary contract are decidedly inferior to those conferred upon the holder of a negotiable instrument. Specifically, the holder of an ordinary contract must be able to prove consideration, whereas, absent evidence to the contrary, consideration is assumed for the holder of a negotiable instrument. Moreover, the holder of an ordinary contract is subject to personal defenses, whereas these defenses are not as easily brought against a holder in due course of a negotiable instrument.

PARTIES ORIGINATING NOTE AND DRAFTS

The parties originating a note are:

- The maker of the note, who promises to pay the note
- The payee, who expects to be paid by the maker.

The parties originating a draft are:

- The drawer of the draft, who promises to pay
- The drawee, who is designated by the drawer to make payment
- The payee, who expects to be paid by the drawer.

CONDITIONS SATISFIED IN ORDER TO BE NEGOTIABLE

An instrument must:

- Be written
- Be signed by the maker or drawer
- Contain an unconditional promise to pay a specified amount of money
- Be payable upon demand or at a specified time
- Be payable either "to order" or "to bearer."

AMBIGUOUS CONDITIONS

For an instrument to be negotiable, all five conditions governing negotiable instruments must be fulfilled. If one or more of these five required conditions is ambiguous, the instrument is deemed to be non-negotiable. In addition, in the event an instrument is determined to be non-negotiable, no agreement among the parties is sufficient to make the instrument negotiable.

UNCONDITIONAL

In relation to elements of negotiability, the term "unconditional" broadly means that the promise or order to pay is not limited or altered by any other item contained within or otherwise incorporated into the instrument.

STATEMENTS IN AN INSTRUMENT

Describe some of the statements that may appear on an instrument that would not destroy its negotiability and identify the two types of statements that can render a negotiable instrument nonnegotiable. Statements that may be contained within or otherwise incorporated into the instrument include: descriptions of the transactions from which the instrument rose, separate writings regarding issues such as prepayment or collateral, and statements by the debtor in which he waives the benefit of laws intended for his benefit. The two types of statements that can render a negotiable instrument non-negotiable are an express condition on payment and a statement that the instrument is governed by another agreement. An instrument that is deemed non-negotiable is not necessarily worthless. It may still reveal a valid, enforceable contract.

RULES OF CONSTRUCTION

The rules of construction for a negotiable instrument include:

- It may be postdated, antedated or undated; it does not have to specify the place where the instrument is drawn or payable.
- Authorized agents may complete an instrument because the rules of agency apply.
- If it is unclear whether the instrument is a draft or a note, the holder of a negotiable instrument may choose which type of instrument it is.
- Two or more persons may sign a negotiable instrument as co-makers or co-drawers; in so doing, each person becomes fully responsible for any liability associated with that role, unless otherwise specified.

PAYABLE ON DEMAND AND PAYABLE AT A DEFINITE TIME

An instrument is deemed payable on demand when the instrument explicitly states that it is payable on demand or otherwise indicates that it is payable at the will of the holder, and additionally does not state a specific time for payment. This type of instrument becomes due upon being presented for payment. To be payable at a definite time, an instrument needs to specify a fixed date (or dates) or a fixed period after presentment or acceptance. However, the payment time cannot be described as being dependent upon the nebulously-defined occurrence of a special event or act, regardless of whether the event or act is bound to occur at some time.

PAYABLE "TO ORDER" OR "TO BEARER"

An instrument is payable "to order" of an identified person, and it is payable only to that person. An instrument is payable "to bearer" when the instrument does not explicitly state a payee and simply states to pay to:

- Bearer
- The order of bearer

- An identified person or bearer; and
- Cash to the order of cash.

Rules Governing Disputes

The rules governing disputes regarding the terms of an instrument are as follows:

- Handwriting is given precedence over typewriting and print.
- Typewriting is given precedence over print.
- Words are given precedence over numbers.
- An unspecified rate of interest is construed as being the same as the interest rate currently in effect at the location where the instrument is paid.

Signatures

While it is not necessary for a signature to be handwritten, a signature, which is defined as any symbol that a party adopts in order to authenticate a writing, must be present on the instrument that the maker intends to be executed. The law presumes that a signature is authentic and authorized; that is, that the signature has been made with the actual, implied, or apparent consent of the party who will be bound by the signature.

Holder in Due Course

A person or institution becomes a holder in due course through the following steps:

1. In return for a person's promise to repay a borrowed sum of money with interest, an original creditor loans that person (now the debtor) money.
2. Then a new creditor, such as a bank or other financial institution, purchases the credit contract from the original creditor.
3. Finally, the new creditor takes the debt, with no knowledge that (a) there exists any defect in the contract; (b) the original creditor has made any misrepresentations to the debtor; and (c) there exists no other act that would enable the debtor to pursue a legal claim against the original creditor.

The new creditor is now the holder in due course and is not responsible for any alleged misdeeds of the original creditor in the original credit transaction.

A holder of a negotiable instrument can become that instrument's holder in due course, depending upon these requirements: (1) the instrument when issued must not contain any evidence of any consideration casting doubt upon the instrument's authenticity (e.g., forgery or alteration); and (2) the holder must take the instrument (a) for value, (b) in good faith, and (c) without knowledge of any apparent defect in the instrument such as the instrument being overdue, containing an unauthorized signature, or having been in some way altered or dishonored.

A holder of a negotiable instrument can become the holder in due course of the instrument if the requirement is fulfilled that the holder must take the instrument for value. If the holder does give value for the note, then and only then, is he a bona fide holder. "Taking for value" refers to three circumstances that can occur: (1) the mutually agreed-upon consideration has been fulfilled; (2) the holder acquires a security interest or lien on the instrument; or (3) a person takes an instrument as security or payment for a previously existing claim.

These are not considered holder in due course "value":

1. Gifts
2. Inheritances
3. Unperformed promises
4. Purchases that are made to satisfy legal proceedings, e.g., foreclosures
5. Bulk transfers made outside the ordinary course of business

The defects that will prevent the holder of a negotiable instrument from becoming a holder in due course are as follows:

1. The instrument is overdue, which can occur in the case of instruments with a specific due date. In this case, some or all of the amount of the instrument remains unpaid after the due date.
2. The instrument is dishonored. An instrument is considered to be dishonored when payment has been refused or when acceptance has not occurred. In the case of a draft, dishonoring is most commonly effected by the drawee; in the case of a note, dishonoring is most commonly effected by the maker.
3. There are defenses against or claims to the instrument. This includes forgeries, improper modifications to the instrument, or evidence that any of the parties to the instrument has obligations that are voidable.

Defenses Against Holders of Due Course

The following are real defenses that work against holders of due course:

- Forgery
- Discharge of the obligor in an insolvency proceeding
- Material alteration of the instrument
- Fraud in the execution

The following are personal defenses that do not work against holders of due course:

- Fraud in the inducement
- Ordinary contract defenses
- Breach of warranty when a draft was accepted
- Non-delivery or unauthorized delivery of an instrument

Restrictions to Protect Consumers

There are certain limitations in particular classes of transactions that the Uniform Commercial Code conveys onto the conferring of a holder of due course. Under section UCC 3-302(g) any laws that favor consumer protection and other public policy concerns override the status afforded a holder in due course. In cases where consumers have personal defenses, the courts in some states have reduced or simply eliminated a holder in due course's right to collect. In cases involving companies with strong relationships to sellers of consumer products, some states have gone so far as to simply eliminate the status afforded a holder in due course.

Attempting to make consumer protections more uniform, in 1976, the Federal Trade Commission addressed concerns about consumer protection, adopting a rule that a consumer credit agreement include (in very bold type) a statement notifying holders of consumer credit contracts that they are "subject to all claims and defenses that the debtor could assert against the seller of goods or services obtained pursuant hereto or with the proceeds hereof." The consequence of this action is to effectively prevent holder in due course status. That is, a debtor or a consumer may offer defenses and claims against not only the seller, but also all subsequent holders.

Good Faith

"Good faith" is most often defined as fairness, honesty, and lawfulness of purpose; additionally it is the absence of any intent to defraud, act maliciously, or take unfair advantage. Article 3 of the UCC defines good faith as "honest in fact and the observance of reasonable commercial standards of fair dealing." Consequently, the holder of a negotiable instrument takes that instrument in good faith if he acts honestly. The test is subjective, which means it is open to interpretation. The holder is acting in good faith depending upon whether the holder believes that the instrument is genuine, authorized, and conforming with the law. There are certain obvious defenses that may result in a presumption against subjective good faith, including the instrument's appearance, the time remaining before the due date and the time and place of the instrument's transfer.

Uniform Commercial Code

Published in 1952, the Uniform Commercial Code attempts to reconcile the laws of sales and other commercial transactions in all 50 states within the United States. This objective is important because most commercial transactions extend beyond one state. The Code is the joint product of the American Law Institute and the National Conference of Commissioners on Uniform State Law. It is not itself the law, but is composed of recommendations of the laws that the authors of the code felt should be adopted in each state. Once enacted by a state's legislature and codified into the state's code of statutes, it becomes actual statutory law. Articles 3 and 4 of the Uniform Commercial Code illuminate law governing the two fundamental types of commercial paper: (1) promises to pay money; and (2) orders to pay money. Article 3 specifically deals with negotiable instruments, whereas Article 4 specifically concerns itself with bank deposits and collections.

Assigning Rights to Another Person

The assignor may be able to transfer his contractual rights to an assignee in an ordinary contract. The assignee in essence assumes the legal role previously held by the assignor, even though the assignee was not a party to the original contract. In accepting these transferred contractual rights, the assignee takes a risk, as he becomes subject to all the contractual defenses to which the assignor had been subject. Due to the assignee assuming these risks, he may request payment for accepting the assignment and may insist on taking a negotiable instrument if possible.

Negotiation

The process known as negotiation relates to the manner in which negotiable paper is transferred from one party to another. The ease and safety of this process confers inherent value on negotiable paper. Naturally, the instrument must be negotiable for negotiation to occur. Negotiation involves both the transfer of possession of the instrument and also the transfer of title to the instrument. The negotiable instrument is transferred to a holder.

The processes by which the following types of negotiable paper are negotiated or transferred are:

- Bearer paper -- Negotiable paper; for example a check made out to "cash" or endorsed in blank, can be negotiated merely by a change of possession, also known as "delivery." ("Endorsed in blank" refers to paper that contains no such clause as "Pay to the order of ___" or "For deposit only.") The disadvantage of bearer paper is its being capable of being transferred to a thief, i.e., someone who is not the lawful owner of the paper.

- Order paper – a negotiable paper that requires both delivery and also the proper endorsements; for a transferee to be awarded rights under an instrument, he must be able to prove not only that the instrument is valid but that he also has a valid claim to it. In other words, in contrast to the case of bearer paper, there are no presumptions in favor of the transferee's claim.

ENDORSEMENTS

An endorsement is the holder's signature on an instrument of negotiable paper. There may be additional or qualifying words accompanying this signature. The result of the endorsement is to transfer the holder's proprietary interest in the negotiable paper to a new holder. An instrument may be endorsed on its front or its back. It can also be endorsed on a paper physically attached to it, which then becomes a part of the negotiable paper called an allonge. In the event that a name on the instrument is misspelled, the holder may write his endorsement as either the correct name or the misspelled name.

The following are different types of endorsements:

- Blank endorsements -- Also known as general endorsements, blank endorsements specify no specific endorsee. Thus, a blank endorsement converts a document of title into a negotiable instrument that is payable to bearer.
- Special endorsements -- This type of endorsement names the endorsee to whom or upon whose order a negotiable instrument is payable.
- Restrictive endorsements -- a type of endorsement further limiting the negotiability of a negotiable instrument, such as "Accounts payee only" and "For deposit only"

PRIMARY AND SECONDARY LIABILITY

Primary parties are those parties who are drawers, makers, and acceptors and are primarily liable on the instrument. Secondary parties as those parties who are endorsers and are secondarily liable on the instrument. Primary parties must pay on an instrument either (1) as the instrument existed when drafted by the drawer or when accepted by the drawee; or (2) in the case of an incomplete instrument, as the instrument exists when ultimately completed. In the case that the primary party has not paid, the secondary party is obliged to pay assuming that (1) the person seeking payment first sought payment from the primary party; and (2) the secondary party was notified that the primary party refused to pay.

NEGLIGENCE

The following are examples of actions by which a party is deemed to be negligent in his duties as a party to an instrument:

1. The party delivers an instrument to the wrong person.
2. The drawer fails to include a corporate designation (e.g., Inc., Corp.) after a corporate name.
3. Corporate books have not been subject to a proper audit.
4. The security of a signature stamp has been compromised.
5. A party fails to act to prevent further forgeries, even after having received notice that forgeries have occurred.

Endorsements Under Payee's Name Used for Negotiation

The three cases under which endorsements under the payee's name are effective for negotiation purposes are:

1. The case of imposters: An imposter causes the drawer or maker of a negotiable instrument to issue the instrument to the imposter or the imposter's accomplice.
2. The case of a fictitious payee: The payee was never intended to have an interest in the instrument, and yet an agent of the drawer or maker supplied the drawer or maker with the payee's name or signed the instrument for the maker or drawer.
3. The case of a trusted employee: An employee of the drawer or maker forges the payee's endorsement on the negotiable instrument, deposits the instrument into an account under the employer's name, but then actually uses the account for his own personal interest.

Presentment Warranty

A presentment warranty is a warranty to which the person accepting or obtaining payment on a negotiable instrument and, additionally, all prior transferors are subject. The three types of warrantees that comprise presentment warranties are:

1. Good title -- occurring when the person and/or prior transferor(s) is entitled to accept or obtain payment for the draft or is authorized to act on behalf of another party who is so entitled
2. No knowledge of forged drawer or maker signature -- occurring when the person and/or prior transferor(s) is unaware that the drawer's signature is forged
3. No material alterations -- only applicable in the case of unaccepted drafts when the instrument has not been altered

Discharge of Liability Other Than Payment

Ways other than payment by which a person's liability to pay an instrument may be discharged include:

- An instrument's cancellation
- Reimbursement rights have been in some way impaired.
- The instrument has been fraudulently altered.
- Acceptance of a draft or check certification
- A former holder reacquires the instrument.
- There has been an unexcused delay in presentment.
- There has been an unexcused delay in notice of dishonor.
- Acceptance varying a draft
- A simple contract to pay money as committed to by any agreement or act

Contract Between a Bank and Depositing Customer

The bank acquires title to the deposited money when it accepts a person's (a customer's) deposit. As a result, the bank becomes the debtor to the account holder, and the account holder becomes the creditor to the bank. The account holder, however, is merely a general creditor, as opposed to a secured party who may seize specific property to pay his account in the event the bank becomes insolvent (although most deposits are insured by the Federal Deposit Insurance Corporation). Since the customer doesn't actually own the bank's funds, he cannot assign these funds, but can only order the bank to make payment by writing a check on his deposited funds.

Bank's Responsibility to Customers

The principal responsibility of a bank to its customers is to honor by making payment on the customer's checks when the customer has sufficient funds in his account to do so. If the bank unintentionally yet mistakenly dishonors a customer's check, the bank is liable to its customers. However, this liability is limited to actual damages, which may include damage to the customer's credit or reputation, arrest, or other proved, consequential damages. A bank also has the responsibility to maintain replicas of customer signatures and to be sufficiently familiar with these signatures to prevent forgeries from going undetected.

Customers' Responsibility to Bank and Preclusion from Asserting Claims

The principle responsibility to the bank of a bank's customer is to ensure that sufficient funds are maintained in his account for the bank to make payment on the checks the customer expects to write. Also, the customer is obliged to do his part in preventing or correcting unauthorized transactions by promptly reviewing his bank statements and other documents (e.g., cancelled checks) sent to him by the bank.

The two situations in which a customer is precluded from asserting a claim against the bank resulting from an alteration or an unauthorized signature are:

1. The bank suffers a loss due to the customer's failure to report an alteration or an unauthorized signature.
2. The bank has paid in good faith and without notice from the customer of the type of problem the customer should have discovered (e.g., repeated forgery by the same person) before the time at which payment was actually made.

Rules Governing the Payment of Checks

The rules governing the payment of checks as stated in Article 4 of the UCC are:

1. The bank is not required to pay overdrafts unless the bank has specifically agreed to do so.
2. In the case of a paid overdraft, the bank may charge the customer for the full amount that the bank has paid.
3. The bank is not required to pay uncertified checks that have been drawn over six months prior to presentation for payment.
4. A bank may supply necessary endorsements for a customer except in the case where the check explicitly requires the payee to sign and the check lacks the payee's endorsement.
5. In the event of a customer's death or incompetence, a bank may continue to honor (pay) his checks until having been notified of the death or incompetence and until the bank has a reasonable opportunity to respond.
6. A customer can issue a stop-payment order, which directs the bank not to pay a particular check.

Certified Check

A non-certified check is only as good as the credit of the drawer. However, a certified check carries the issuing bank's guarantee. A bank is not required to certify a check, but its refusal to certify is not an indication of the check's dishonor, but rather indicates that the bank has not agreed in advance to cover the check. When the bank does agree to issue a certified check, it guarantees that the certified check will (1) have an authorized signature; and (2) be paid when presented for payment. The issuing bank takes out the check's amount from the drawer's account and holds the amount in reserve, thus ensuring the check's payment. A certified check is the equivalent of cash, and its payment cannot be prevented by a stop-payment order. The drawer and all endorsers prior to certification are released from liability on the check once the check is certified.

Alteration of Certified Checks

The general rules governing the situation where the drawer of a check was not negligent, but the check was altered are:

1. To the extent of the increased amount, the bank bears a loss.
2. The bank may charge the drawer for the original amount of the check.
3. The bank may hold liable the person who presented the check for payment.

The critical issue when a certified check has been altered is when the alteration took place. If the check had been altered prior to certification, the alterations are considered to have been accepted by the certifying bank. However, the certifying bank cannot be expected to have accepted alterations that occurred after the check was certified and will only be held liable for the original amount of the check.

Electronic Funds Transfer Act of 1978

The considerations addressed in the Electronic Funds Transfer Act of 1978 include:

- Customer liability is limited for a lost or stolen bank card.
- Customers must be provided with receipts for computer terminal transactions (typically ATM transactions).
- Banks are required to provide a statement for each month in which an electronic transfer occurs.
- It is the customer's responsibility to discover any errors on the monthly statement and to notify his bank within 60 days.
- Customers must be provided with information about the rules and duties under the Electronic Funds Transfer Act if they are opening electronic funds transfer accounts.

Important Terms

Commercial paper -- documents whose purpose is to help bring about the transfer of either money or credit; also, promissory notes that have short to very short maturity periods and secured solely by the issuer's reputation

Promissory note -- a written, signed, unconditional, and unsecured promise that pledges one party (the maker or "promisor") to pay a specified sum on demand; the promissory note can also commit that specified sum to be paid on a fixed or decided date to another party (the payee or "promisee").

Negotiation -- the process of transferring possession and title to an instrument from one party to another

Holder -- a party who possesses a document of title, a negotiable instrument, or a security that is drawn, issued, or endorsed to the party

Holder – the person possessing a negotiable instrument that is issued, drawn or endorsed to that person or to his order as bearer

Holder in due course -- the person who takes possession of a negotiable instrument, such as a promissory note for value, lacking knowledge of any apparent defect in the instrument or any notice of dishonor

Assignor -- the party to an ordinary contract who assigns to someone else his rights under the contract

Assignee -- the party to an ordinary contract to whom the assignor assigns his rights under the contract

Accommodation party -- A person who, for the purpose of lending his credit status so that another person can secure a necessary loan or other arrangement, has signed an instrument in some capacity, for example as a maker, drawer, or acceptor, without receiving value for it. Thus, the accommodation party is subject to enforcement of the instrument by subsequent holders for value.

Guarantor -- a person who guarantees to pay someone else's debt if he or she should default on a loan obligation via a statement to the effect of "payment guaranteed". In other words, the above statement by the guarantor converts his secondary liability status to one of primary liability.

Legal Environment

Ethical Rules for Attorneys

Attorneys are governed by the Model Rules of Professional Conduct set forth by the American Bar Association. The ethical rules for attorneys are clear and may be different from what a person would associate with typically accepted ethics. For example, if a private person heard a murder confession, ethics may dictate that he report such a confession to the police, while if an attorney hears such a confession, ethical rules dictate that he is not permitted to reveal the information due to attorney/client privilege. An attorney who fails to abide by the Rules of Professional Conduct can be subject to disciplinary sanctions, up to and including the loss of his license to practice law.

Power to Regulate Businesses

The US Constitution gives the federal government the power to regulate businesses in the Commerce Clause in Article I, Section 8, Clause 3. Because the federal government has only enumerated powers, and all other powers are reserved to the state, this clause was essential to allow the government to regulate businesses. The clause gives the federal government the power "to regulate Commerce with foreign Nations, and among the several States, and with the Indian Tribes." This means that any business decision or activity that may have an impact on commerce among the states is subject to federal government regulation. The Commerce Clause has been interpreted broadly to allow for widespread federal regulation. It is from the Commerce Clause that the federal government obtains the power to pass anti-trust laws, as well as food, product, and safety laws.

Publicly-Held Companies

Publicly-held companies are owned by shareholders, and when the companies are traded on a stock market any individual can make a purchase of that company. Because shareholders are part owners of a company, they are entitled to protections and are entitled to have the corporate officers and staff working for their best interests and on their behalf. With privately-held companies, the owners also generally manage the company. Because no widespread public interest is at stake and because the owners generally have more control, there are less stringent laws and protections in place to protect owners of privately-held companies.

Disclosures

Publicly-held companies must release quarterly earnings statements that indicate their earnings per share. Publicly-held companies must also release disclosures to shareholders regarding their profits and losses, the amount of liquid assets they have, and any debt that they have incurred. When a company executive such as a corporate officer or board member exercises stock options or sells stock, this also must be disclosed to the public. The reason for mandated disclosures is to protect the interests of those who invest in publicly-held companies and to ensure that they have sufficient financial information about the company to make an educated investing decision.

Piercing the Corporate Veil

A corporation acts as a separate legal entity and, as a general matter, officers and managers of a corporation cannot be held legally accountable for debts or lawsuits or judgments against the corporation. "Piercing the corporate veil" occurs when an individual is personally held liable for the activities or behavior of his company and his personal assets may be used to satisfy judgments or debts. "Piercing the corporate veil" is appropriate only when the corporate officer and the corporation were substantially the same and/or where there was a substantial intermingling of personal and corporate assets.

Administrative Agencies

Administrative agencies are established in order to ensure compliance with various pieces of legislation designed to regulate business. Many of the regulations to regulate businesses, such as Civil Rights laws and the Fair Labor Standards Act, contain hundreds of pages of provisions, rules, and regulations. These agencies are created in order to explain and more clearly define issues that arise from existing business legislation and to enforce the rules and regulations imposed upon businesses.

EPA

The Environmental Protection Agency, or EPA, is the administrative agency vested with the responsibility of enforcing various pieces of environmental protection legislation. The EPA was created by President Richard Nixon in 1970, and oversees and enforces acts related to air pollution, water pollution, land pollution, hazardous waste, and endangered species. Examples of acts enforced by the EPA include the Clean Air Act, the Toxic Substances Control Act, the Water Quality Act, the Safe Drinking Water Act, the Solid Waste Disposal Act, and the Endangered Species Preservation Act, among others.

Air Pollution Control Act

The Air Pollution Control Act was passed in 1955, and was the first of a series of measures passed by Congress designed to control air pollution. The Act vested the power in the federal government, mandating that the US Surgeon General had the authority to investigate and make decisions about the reduction in air pollution. The Act was later amended in 1963 with the Clean Air Act which widened the authoritative power of Congress to actually impose limitations on emissions of noxious and hazardous gases into the air.

Toxic Substances Control Act

The Toxic Substances Control Act was passed in 1976 to provide the federal government with the authority to regulate the introduction and distribution of chemicals. The Toxic Substances Control Act mandates that the government may maintain a list of approved chemicals, as well as prohibit chemicals not on the list. The Act also sets standards that chemicals must meet and safety tests and provisions that a chemical must undergo before it can be added to the list of approved chemicals. Chemicals on the list are both toxic and non-toxic. Limitations may also be imposed regarding the distribution and use of approved chemicals.

Clean Water Act

The Clean Water Act was passed in 1977 as an amendment to earlier legislation- the Water Pollution Control Act and the Federal Water Pollution Control Amendments of 1972. The Clean Water Act is enforced by the EPA and prohibits the release of chemicals and other items into water, including ground water. All navigable waters are covered by the Clean Water Act and the Act mandates that permits must be obtained from all point sources (industrial facilities, government buildings, agricultural facilities, and other areas who release items into water) before any chemicals or items can be released. The Act is designed to protect and preserve drinking water as well as oceans, lakes and streams.

Federal Insecticide, Fungicide, and Rodenticide Act

The Federal Insecticide, Fungicide, and Rodenticide Act of 1972 sets forth the basic rules in regards to pesticide regulation in the United States. It grants the Environmental Protection Agency (EPA) with the authority to oversee and manage the approval and use of different pesticides. This Act also sets standards by which pesticides are tested both to achieve their relevant goals of eliminating pests, as well as standards by which pesticides must be tested to be safe for use around humans.

Endangered Species Protection Act

The Endangered Species Protection Act was passed in 1966, and gave the Secretary of the Interior the right to research and to take steps to protect endangered species and wildlife which are at risk of extinction. The Act also vested the Secretary of the Interior with the authority to manage a National Wildlife Refuge system which was designed to create habitats and assist animals in danger of becoming extinct. This was later followed by the Endangered Species Act which put additional restrictions on the hunting of endangered species and limited the destruction of habitat vital to the existence of endangered species.

Solid Waste Disposal Act

The Solid Waste Disposal Act was passed in 1965 and allowed the federal government and the Environmental Protection Agency with control over the disposal of certain types of waste. The Solid Waste Disposal Act provided a definition of hazardous or dangerous wastes and set forth rules by which waste could be disposed. Reporting requirements were put in place to ensure that companies comply with rules and do not dispose of solid waste in a manner that is likely to harm the soil or ground water.

Resource Conservation and Recovery Act

The Resource Conservation and Recovery Act passed in 1976 and expanded the Solid Waste Disposal Act of 1965. The Resource Conservation and Recovery Act gave the government greater authority to deal with the disposal of industrial and hazardous wastes. Under the Resource Conservation and Recovery Act, hazardous materials are tracked from their production to their disposal to ensure that no hazardous wastes are ever improperly disposed. The Act also imposes regulations for non-hazardous solid waste, such as automobile tires and household garbage, placing limits on the locations where such waste may be disposed.

Environmental Impact Statement

An environmental impact statement must be prepared by a government entity or organization before it conducts a project that is likely to have any impact on the environment. The requirements for an environmental impact statement were set forth in the National Environmental Policy Act and stipulate that the statement must explain any and all impact on ground water, animal habitats, and air quality before a project is undertaken.

Conservation Easement

A conservation easement is a grant of land by a landowner to the government that separates ownership rights from the right to develop the property. The owner of the land may designate a certain area, providing an easement to the government or other entity which gives the government the right to restrict the development of that particular land. The landowner still maintains full ownership rights but cannot cut down trees or otherwise develop the land. The purpose is to preserve scenic open spaces, natural resources, and wildlife habitats. A landowner who grants a conservation easement generally receives tax benefits for doing so.

Vehicle Emissions Laws

Emission is the amount of gases produced by a vehicle that can be hazardous to air quality. The majority of states within the United States require a car to pass emissions inspections on an annual, biannual, or other routine basis. In such cases, a test is performed to ensure that the car does not emit more noxious gases than is normal. The major purpose of emissions laws is to protect the quality of the air and to minimize the impact of transportation vehicles in light of the concern about global warming. States can pass their own individual emissions laws concerning vehicles registered within their borders.

Comprehensive Environmental Response, Compensation, and Liability Act

The Comprehensive Environmental Response, Compensation, and Liability Act passed in 1980 and established a superfund that will pay for toxic cleanup and abandoned hazardous waste sites. Under the Superfund Act, the federal government can spend the money to clean up a toxic waste site. If the owner is later identified, he must reimburse the superfund the money spent for the cleanup, in addition to fees and penalties. Both removal of toxic waste and remedial action to minimize the impact of toxic waste is paid for under the Superfund, which was passed in response to the Love Canal disaster in which toxic waste sites made citizens very ill.

Proving Injury in Environmental Cases

Often, the damage from exposure to environmental toxins does not show up for many years. It also shows up in the form of cancer or other illnesses of which it may not be easy to prove the cause. Since a plaintiff may have difficulty showing that the exposure to pollution and toxins caused the injury, it can be difficult to prove the proximate cause component of a negligence case, and it can also be difficult to prove that the plaintiff suffered damages as a result of the exposure to the environmental toxin.

Injury Due to Disposal of Hazardous Wastes

Various laws ensure that manufacturers and industrial plants appropriately dispose of wastes. For example, Clean Water Acts require companies to obtain a permit before disposing of anything into groundwater, while hazardous waste regulations track hazardous waste from production to disposal. If a company fails to follow required provisions, the company can be fined. If a company's actions cause damage to a person, that private citizen or group of people can sue the company to recover monetary compensation for his loss. Thus, a company is subject to both sanctions from the government, as well as civil sanctions.

SEC

The Securities and Exchange Commission (SEC) is responsible for ensuring compliance with Securities law in the US The SEC investigates allegations of insider trading or other improprieties associated with issuing or trading securities (stocks). The SEC can bring criminal charges against a company or entity found or suspected to be in violation of securities laws. The SEC also sets and enforces rules for the disclosure of public companies, enforces accounting standards, and otherwise monitors investments and activities of public companies with the goal of protecting the general rights of shareholders.

FTC

The Fair Trade Commission, or FTC, is the Federal Agency vested with the responsibility of ensuring a free market system and fair competition. The FTC enforces anti-trust legislation and brings lawsuits to stop mergers or acquisitions that may violate anti-trust principles. The FTC also enforces rules against price fixing and other consumer protection legislation, such as predatory pricing.

Monopoly

A monopoly occurs when one organization, entity, or group of entities corners an entire market for a given substance or item. Monopolies are illegal because they can give rise to predatory behavior.

If there is only one paint supplier in the world or one group of paint suppliers in the world, then those suppliers could get together and decide to charge astronomical prices for paint. Customers would then have to pay the higher price since no other options for paint exist. Prohibitions against monopolies are designed to ensure free market competition so the economic rules of supply and demand can result in fair prices in line with the market's demand for the product.

Clayton Act

The Clayton Antitrust Act was passed in 1914 to prohibit the formation of trusts. Trusts are groups of organizations or entities that band together to create an anti-competitive monopoly. For example, if all the airlines got together and decided to set minimum prices in order to make air travel more expensive, this would be an example of an illegal trust. The Act prohibits price discrimination or price fixing, the creation of a monopoly by the purchase and/or acquisition or merger with all competitors, and exclusive sales agreements. The Clayton Act was an addition to earlier anti-trust legislation such as the Sherman Act.

Sherman Act

The Sherman Antitrust Act was passed in 1890 and was the first federal rule against monopolies and trusts designed to preserve the free market and competition. The Act vests the federal government with the authority to investigate any companies that are suspected of violating rules against monopolies, price fixing, or other anti-competitive activities. It also prohibits the restriction of supply in order to artificially raise prices and limits mergers that would result in monopolies.

Antitrust Law

Antitrust law is the body of law that prohibits the formation of monopolies or other anticompetitive practices. It is so named because monopolies were often held in trust in past times, although today there is little meaning to the word "trust" as far as monopolistic or anticompetitive activity is concerned. Antitrust laws prohibit any and all behavior from monopolies to price fixing to predatory pricing that would interfere with a free market system. This is important because economists believe that in a free market where no monopolies or anti-competitive prices exist, the supply and demand meet at an appropriate point on a curve, and the price will be best determined by the point at which supply and demand meet.

Price Fixing

Price fixing occurs when one or more companies agree to set a price at or above a certain level instead of allowing the market to set a price. In order to achieve a free market system, price fixing is prohibited in the United States. One example of price fixing would occur if every bakery in town got together at a meeting and decided that no one single bakery would price their muffins below $1.00. The price would thus be artificially inflated based on the bakers' agreement.

Insider Trading

Insider trading occurs when a person with advanced knowledge of what a publicly- held company will do uses that knowledge to his financial advantage in order to buy or sell stocks. Insider trading is prohibited because it hurts the average investor who is not privy to the insider information. This can affect the price of a stock causing it to rise or fall on the basis of the insider information, thus affecting the value of the average investors' profits. Insider trading also gives rise to market manipulation and other illegal activities that would occur when those with insider information act to cause the price of a stock to behave in a certain way.

Anti-Discrimination Legislation

The federal government regulates employment discrimination in Title VII of the Civil Rights Act of 1964. Title VII prohibits discrimination on the basis of race, color, national origin, gender, or religion. The Age Discrimination in Employment Act prohibits discrimination on the basis of being aged 40 or over. The Americans with Disabilities Act prohibits discrimination on the basis of being disabled.

Protected Classes Regarding Employment Discrimination

Title VII of the Civil Rights Act of 1964 establishes race, religion, gender, national origin, and color as protected classes. The Age Discrimination in Employment Act makes those over the age of 40 a protected class. The Americans with Disabilities Act makes those who suffer a disability that inhibits or interferes with their daily activities a protected class. Discrimination is not illegal unless it is against a protected class. For example, it is illegal to fire someone because she is a woman or to fire someone because he is a man. Therefore, these are protected classes. It is not illegal to fire someone who is unattractive, so unattractive people are not a protected class.

Affirmative Action

Affirmative action permits limited discrimination on the basis of race or national origin in order to give an advantage to those underrepresented minorities. This is common in school admissions and can also be used as criteria for jobs. However, the 2003 *Grutter v. Bollinger* case stated that although affirmative action was appropriate, quotas in which a specific number or set advantage is given to people of minority races are not permitted.

Title VII of Civil Rights Act of 1964

Title VII of the Civil Rights Act of 1964 prohibits discrimination in the hiring, firing, terms, and conditions of employment. This means that a person cannot be treated any differently in any aspect of his employment from promotion to pensions to the location of his office on the basis of race, gender, color, national origin, or religion. A person also cannot be made to feel uncomfortable or inferior on the basis of his protected status, and the employer must make reasonable accommodations if necessary on the basis of the protected status, such as allowing a religious person to adhere to his religious principles as long as the principles do not unreasonably interfere with the person's work.

Hostile Work Environment

A hostile work environment is prohibited by anti-discrimination laws such as Title VII. A hostile work environment is an environment in which a person is made to feel uncomfortable or treated differently at work on the basis of his age, race, religion, gender, color, national origin, or disability. If a woman is subject to continual exposure to sexual innuendo and made uncomfortable by the placement of inappropriate sexual pictures around the office, this is an example of a hostile work environment. An employer can be held legally liable for any damage a plaintiff suffers on the basis of a hostile work environment.

Quid Pro Quo Sexual Harassment

Quid pro quo sexual harassment is the type of sexual harassment that most people think of when they think of sexual harassment. This type of harassment trades sexual favors for promotions or other benefits of employment. For example, if a woman is told she will be promoted only if she sleeps with her boss or is threatened with a salary cut if she doesn't go out on a date with her co-worker, then this exemplifies quid pro quo sexual harassment.

DIFFERENCE FROM HOSTILE WORK ENVIRONMENT CASES

In a case of sexual harassment in which a hostile work environment is created, the person being sexually harassed need not have been offered any benefits or enticements in exchange for sex. Instead, he or she must have merely been made to feel uncomfortable or put into an uncomfortable situation on the basis of his or her sex. For example, being subject to sexual jokes or being exposed to pornographic images at work after expressing a desire for this not to occur exemplifies a hostile work environment. Quid pro quo harassment, on the other hand, occurs when a person is offered a promotion or job benefit if he or she engages in sexual activities or behavior.

DISPARATE IMPACT

Disparate impact occurs if a job qualification or condition unfairly discriminates against a protected class and does not have a legitimate job benefit. For example, an employer cannot make climbing stairs a prerequisite of employment to prohibit those in a wheelchair from going to work for the company unless climbing stairs is a bona fide and essential part of the job. Likewise, if a pre-employment test results in the elimination of the majority of candidates of a specific race, then the test may be considered to have a disparate impact and may be prohibited unless the employer can prove a legitimate occupational reason for the test that cannot be met in another manner with less disparate impact.

BONA FIDE OCCUPATIONAL QUALIFICATION

A bona fide occupational qualification is a qualification that is required for a job and is used to determine whether a given company is unfairly or illegally discriminating. For example, it may be a bona fide occupational qualification for a church to demand that its minister be of a certain religion. Therefore, it would not be considered religious discrimination if that church refused to hire a minister who was of a different religion. To be a bona fide occupational qualification, the qualification must be necessary to the performance of the job. It would not, for example, be a bona fide occupational qualification that the lunch lady in a church necessarily be the same religion as the church, so it may not be appropriate and may be illegal to discriminate on the basis of religion when hiring a church lunch lady.

EMPLOYMENT DISCRIMINATION CASE

In order to prove employment discrimination, the plaintiff must first prove that he or she is a member of a protected class. The plaintiff then must prove that the defendant employer discriminated in the terms, conditions, or hiring and firing process on the basis of his protected status. Finally, the plaintiff must prove that he suffered damages including lost wages and/or emotional distress as a result of the discrimination.

AT-WILL EMPLOYMENT

At-will employment is the rule in the vast majority of situations in the United States, unless an individual or employer opts out of at-will employment through the creation of an employment contract. Under the doctrine of at-will employment, any employee can be hired or fired, and any employee can quit at any time for any reason. The only limitations to at-will employment exist in the form of anti-discrimination legislation which mandates that an employee cannot be fired on the basis of his race, gender, religion, color, national origin, age, or disability.

REASONABLE ACCOMMODATIONS

Employers are required to make reasonable accommodations in order to allow a disabled person to work and in order to accommodate the religious freedom of employees. Reasonable accommodations are determined on a case-by-case basis in light of the cost of the potential accommodation and the adverse impact on other employees and on the company as a result of the accommodations. For example, it would likely be considered reasonable accommodations to permit an employee to pray quietly at his desk for five minutes of every hour to accommodate his religious freedom, but it would likely not be considered a reasonable accommodation to permit an employee to slaughter a chicken in religious sacrifice at his desk every day because of the adverse impact such an activity would have on other employees.

Worker's Compensation

The workers compensation system exists as a compulsory alternative to the tort law system that exists within every state of the United States. States pass worker's compensation acts mandating that all employers purchase worker's compensation insurance. When an employee is injured, he recovers for lost wages and medical bills and is otherwise compensated for his injury through that insurer instead of through suing in tort. Worker's compensation is a no-fault system which means a worker can recover money without proving his employer was negligent, as long as the injury occurred in the line of work and the worker was not drunk or otherwise violating express employee guidelines for behavior.

Overtime Regulations

The Fair Labor Standards Act mandates that employees be paid overtime at the rate of time-and-a-half for every hour over 40 hours worked per week. The Act is designed to ensure that employees are not made to work extremely long hours without being fairly compensated and to otherwise ensure that employees are not taken advantage of. Certain exceptions exist for salaried employees. In addition, states can pass more stringent overtime laws in conjunction with the Fair Labor Standards Act, such as rules that any time over eight hours in a single day be counted as overtime work.

Agency Law within Employment Law

Agency law makes a principal vicariously liable for the actions of an agent. For example, if a company instructs an employee to do something and the thing that it instructed the employee to do causes injury, the company may be liable. This means that a company can be held liable for actions of its employees that are carried out in the line of duty. It also means that, since an employee is acting as the agent of the employer, the employee has a fiduciary duty to act in the best interests of the employer.

Employee Duties

An employee acts as an agent of the employer and thus has a fiduciary duty to the employer. The employee cannot divert income that should be given to the employer, nor can the employee take advantage of business opportunities that should rightfully belong to the employer. Under the Faithless Service doctrine, an employee who takes a business opportunity that rightfully belongs to his employer can be divested of all compensation from the job as well as the money he earned through taking the business from his employer.

Employer Liability

Under the doctrine of vicarious liability, any time an employee is acting in the interests of his employer or under the direction of his employer, the employer can be held liable for his actions. If an agent or employee deviates from doing work- referred to as a frolic or detour- vicarious liability ends. For example, if an employee runs an errand for his boss and injures someone with the vehicle, the employer can be vicariously liable since the employee caused the injury in the course of duty. If the employee stops for lunch on the way to run the errand and injures someone on his way to lunch, this may be considered a frolic or detour since the employee was not going to lunch on behalf of his employer.

Secured and Unsecured Loans

A secured loan is a loan for which an asset acts as collateral. A car loan and a mortgage loan are both secured loans, with the car and the house acting as the collateral for each respective loan. An unsecured loan is money given to the borrower to purchase anything he likes with no specific asset(s) used as collateral. Most credit cards are unsecured loans because the person who uses the card can buy anything he wants, and the things he buys won't necessarily have the value of the amount borrowed. With a secured loan, if the borrower does not pay, the creditor can seize the asset which acts as the security in order to satisfy the loan.

Usury

Usury is an interest rate that is absurdly high. The federal government's only regulations against usury come in the form of the RICO act which stipulates that it is a federal offense to lend money at more than two and a half times the state usury rate. Most usury laws are set at a state level and set a maximum interest rate that can be charged for loans. The laws are designed to ensure that creditors will not set astronomically or prohibitively high interest rates that render the borrowers unable to repay the debt.

Creditors' Rights Regarding Bankruptcy

Creditors have a right to appear at bankruptcy proceedings and make claims on the estate. Depending on the type of bankruptcy, creditors also have other rights as well. For example, in a Chapter 7 bankruptcy, creditors have the right to payment from the sale of assets by the trustee. In a Chapter 13 bankruptcy, creditors have the right to review and approve a payment plan proposed by the bankrupt person prior to the courts approving the bankruptcy and settlement. In some cases, creditors also have the right to force a person or entity into involuntary bankruptcy so the court can arrange for the sale of assets by a trustee in order to raise capital to provide payment to creditors.

Limitations on Debt Collection

The Fair Debt Collection Practices Act imposes various limitations on the actions of creditors within the United States. For example, if a debtor requests in writing the proof of a debt, the creditor must send this proof within 30 days or must cease collection activities. A creditor must also not call a debtor outside of certain hours, such as early in the morning or late at night, and must not make threats of legal action unless the creditor actually intends to follow through with the legal action. Finally, once a debt has been discharged in bankruptcy or once the statute of limitations on a debt (normally seven years) has expired, a creditor must not continue debt collection practices.

Chapter 7 and Chapter 13 Bankruptcy

Under Chapter 7 bankruptcy, certain assets are seized and sold. These assets are used to pay creditors. All debts not paid with the sale of assets are forgiven and are no longer collectable. There are exceptions for student loans and unpaid tax debt which may not be eliminated in any type of bankruptcy except in cases of extreme hardship, but generally Chapter 7 bankruptcy provides the debtor with a clean slate. In Chapter 13 bankruptcy, debtors must repay some or all of their debts under a payment plan mandated and enforced by the court. To qualify for Chapter 7 bankruptcy, a debtor's income and assets must be below a certain level (normally the median income for the state) and/or a means test must be passed to determine the amount of disposable income of the debtor.

Non-Recourse Loan

A non-recourse loan is a type of secured loan that limits the debt collection activities to the seizure of collateral. In some states, mortgages are non-recourse loans. This means that if a borrower does not make his mortgage payments, the lender can foreclose on his home but cannot go after any other assets or obtain a judgment in court to satisfy any unpaid balance that remains on the mortgage loan after the home is seized and sold.

Deficiency Judgment

A deficiency judgment is permitted after a foreclosure action in certain states. A foreclosure occurs when a homeowner does not pay his mortgage bills and the lender seizes the home, which was acting as collateral. The home is sold and the bank uses the proceeds from the sale of the home to pay off the remaining balance. If the sale of the home does not generate the full amount necessary to pay off the mortgage, the bank can obtain a deficiency judgment in which the court mandates that the homeowner pay any remaining balance on the loan.

Foreclosure and Repossession

Foreclosure occurs when a home mortgage, secured by a house as collateral, is defaulted. The lender can foreclose and seize the home to sell it in order to recover the balance of the money owed. In some cases, judicial foreclosure is required which means the lender must go to the bank to obtain a judgment of foreclosure. In other cases, the mortgage documents contain a clause permitting the lender to foreclose automatically. Repossession, on the other hand, is the seizure of assets for a secured loan other than a mortgage. For example, a car may be repossessed if the borrower defaults on a car loan.

Product Liability Cases

Standards

Product liability cases can either be judged by a negligence standard or under the doctrine of strict liability. Under a negligence standard, a plaintiff who wishes to recover damage as a result of being injured by a product must prove that the seller or manufacturer was negligent or careless in the production, distribution, or sale of the product and that this negligence led to injury. Many states, however, have adopted a strict liability standard in which a plaintiff does not have to prove negligence. He merely must prove that he was using the project as was intended and was injured by it.

Proving a Product Liability Case

A plaintiff must prove that he used the product as intended. He must prove that the product, when used as intended, was the proximate or direct cause of compensable injury. Finally, he must prove that he suffered actual damages such as pain and suffering, lost wages, and/or emotional distress. In some cases where strict liability does not apply, the plaintiff must also prove that the manufacturer was negligent in the creation or sale of the product and that this negligence led to injury. This is not always required, however.

Class Action Lawsuit

Often, a product will be defective but it won't be worthwhile for each individual customer to pay the legal fees and take the time to sue. In order to ensure the company is still penalized for the defective product and that buyers are compensated, class action lawsuits allow groups of plaintiff to join together to sue. For example, when Apple Computers released iPods with defective batteries, each individual customer would not have found it worthwhile to sue. A class action suit was brought on behalf of all iPod owners, however, so the company was held accountable and each owner received either a $50 credit or free repair of his iPod.

Strict Liability

Strict liability is a stringent standard imposed on manufacturers and sellers of products. It stipulates that if a product injures someone when it is used as intended, the manufacturer and/or seller and all manufacturers of parts can be held legally liable for damages, even if they did not breach a duty of care in the assembly, manufacture, design, or sale of the product. This standard encourages the manufacturers and sellers of items to ensure thorough and careful safety standards and testing measures are in place, since these manufactures will be held accountable any time injury occurs as a result of the use of their product.

Strict liability is used as the standard for product liability in some states because states want to hold companies accountable and ensure companies use thorough and stringent safety standards. A manufacturer of a product is in the best position to perform testing to ensure its product is safe. The manufacturer is also in the best person to hold responsible for injury that occurs if the product is not safe. By imposing liability even in cases where there is no negligence, the law encourages companies thoroughly make sure that people cannot possibly be hurt by the product. It also ensures that those who are hurt are fairly compensated.

Implied Warranty of Merchantability

Implied warranty of merchantability is a legal concept that stipulates that a product must be fit for the use for which it was intended. In other words, a baby stroller must work to transport a baby and must be safe to do so, while a hair dryer must work to dry hair. If a product does not function as intended, the purchaser of the product is entitled to recover damages or financial loss that resulted from the faulty product.

Premises Liability Law

Premises liability law is a body of law designed to ensure that owners of land or buildings make and keep those land and buildings safe. Premises liability law sets the standard of care for the upkeep of different types of premises and environments. For example, people who run a public business are required to keep the premises safe and utterly free of hazards for consumers. Those who own a home are also required to make sure the home is reasonably safe for visitors, but are held to less stringent standards than a public business would be held.

Invitee

Invitee is a classification under premises liability law. Invitees are people who are invited to a premises solely or primarily for the benefit and gain of the premises owner. For example, if someone owns a store and has people come into that store, those people who come to the store are primarily there for the benefit of the owner; the owner needs the customers so the store can be profitable. The highest standard of care is imposed for invitees. Premises' owners who have invitees must ensure that their premises is free of hazards and must warn of any and all hazards that are not reparable or fixable.

Licensee

Licensee is a classification under premises liability law. Licensees are those who enter a premise for the mutual benefit of the premise owner and the visitor. Licensees are granted less protection than invitees, which are those people invited to enter a premises solely for the benefit of the premises owner, but do have more protection than trespassers who are not invited to enter a premises at all.

If a person owns a premises to which licensees come that person must fix serious dangers and warn of any unrepaired dangers, whether obvious or not.

TRESPASSER

Trespassers are a classification under premises liability law. Trespassers are individuals who enter a property solely for their own gain and who are not invited to do so by the owner of the premises. Under the law, trespassers are given very little legal protection, but they are afforded some. A premises owner, for example, cannot set a dangerous trap for trespassers such as creating a hidden hole that trespassers will fall through or planting landmines that trespassers will activate. Non-obvious and life-threatening dangers must also contain warnings.

INTERNATIONAL LAW

When doing business internationally, a business must be aware that different legal standards may apply in different countries. For example, a company that exports food must comply with any and all food safety laws in the country to which it is exporting that food. International businesses must also understand restrictions on trade, tariffs or taxes imposed on imports, and rules regarding which items must be declared to customs officials in the given country. Other issues in international law may include varying legal stances on bribery within different countries, as well as the need to comply with different wage and hour standards in the local economy in which a business operates.

NAFTA

NAFTA, or the North American Free Trade Agreement, passed in 1994 to replace the Canada-United States Free Trade Agreement. NAFTA is an agreement between Canada, the United States, and Mexico to create a tri-lateral trade bloc. NAFTA was designed to eliminate trade barriers, such as tariffs, on trade between the United States, Mexico, and Canada. With the elimination of approximately half of all imports from Mexico and over one-third of US exports to Mexico, it made it more financially advantageous for companies to do business among the three countries. NAFTA also contains provisions to ensure that free trade among the three countries causes no adverse environmental effects.

The tariffs were phased out gradually from NAFTA's passing in 1994 until 2008. Although quantifying the exact effects of NAFTA is difficult due to the complexities of economic growth and trade, most economists believe that NAFTA has made the economies of all three countries more efficient and productive because of the newfound ability to take advantage of economies of scale.

TRADE RESTRICTIONS

Trade restrictions are laws and rules designed to discourage trade among different countries. Trade restrictions can occur in the form of tariffs or taxes on either imports or exports, or on direct rules such as a trade embargo preventing one country from trading with another. For example, as of 2010, the United States embargoes goods from Cuba. Trade restrictions discourage international trade in order to increase products grown and produced within a country. This can be beneficial for some companies within a country who would be unable to compete with lower prices that result from the lower cost of labor in developing countries. However, other countries would do better if trade restrictions were lifted so they could take advantage of a global marketplace.

GATT

The General Agreement on Tariffs and Trade (GATT) is an international treaty relating to how imports and exports will be taxed as they are traded from country to country. The General Agreement on Tariffs and Trade was negotiated by members of the UN during a conference on trade and employment. It was negotiated when members of the UN failed to agree to create an

International Trade Organization. GATT was first created in 1947, but was discontinued when the World Trade Organization (the WTO) was created in 1994. Although the WTO now regulates international trade rules and tariffs, it has employed many of the principles set forth in the original GATT agreement.

WTO

The World Trade Organization was created in 1995 under the Marrakech Agreement. Prior to the creation of the World Trade Organization, the General Agreement on Tariffs and Trade controlled international trade among members of the United Nations (UN). The World Trade Organization, or WTO, now sets standards in order to make international trade more open and to ensure the protection of both international trade and the interests of local businesses, governments, and economies. The WTO regulates trade between countries and helps countries to formalize and create trade agreements and resolve trade disputes.

Functions: The World Trade Organization administers trade agreements between countries. The WTO may review an agreement regulating international trade or may help two countries to create their own agreement governing the trade between them. The WTO also oversees and assists with the implementation of any agreements relating to trade, such as tariffs and free trade agreements. When a dispute arises, the WTO sets forth the appropriate framework by which the countries can amicably resolve their dispute.

Torts

TORTS

Torts are civil wrongs that allow a private party to sue another private party who has caused damage. Under the law of the United States, all individuals are guaranteed the rights to life, liberty, and the pursuit of happiness. If one private individual interferes with the legal rights of another individual, either negligently or intentionally, tort law provides a means by which the damaged individual can sue. Tort law is largely grounded in English common law and American common law, although uniform codes and systems of Tort law have been adopted by some states. Tort penalties are largely monetary.

TORT LAW AND CRIMINAL LAW

Tort law is a civil lawsuit between two parties, while criminal law is a branch of law that allows an officer of the court to enforce conducts and standards of behavior for the benefit of all society. One particular action may subject someone to both criminal and civil liability. For example, if a person is driving his car drunk and injures someone, he may be subject to criminal charges for drunk driving. He may also be sued in a civil case by the person whom he injured, and he may have to pay monetary damages to the victim. The standard of proof and the trials for the civil and criminal cases are entirely separate legal proceedings. For example, O.J. Simpson was found innocent of killing his wife in criminal court, but in civil court the jury determined that he likely had killed his wife and ordered him to pay damages for wrongful death.

INTENTIONAL TORTS AND NEGLIGENT TORTS

Intentional torts are lawsuits that arise when someone is intentionally injured by a tortfeasor. For example, if a person assaults a victim on purpose, the victim can sue for the intentional tort of assault and can recover damages. Negligent torts, on the other hand, occur when a tortfeasor breaches the standard of care that a reasonable person would employ and his carelessness causes injury. The victim in such cases can still sue to recover damages, but he does so under principles of negligence theory instead of suing for an intentional tort.

PROVING INTENTIONAL TORTS

To prove an intentional tort, the plaintiff must first prove that the defendant intended the action that caused the injury. He does not have to prove the victim intended the injury. For example, if Mike intended to throw a rock at Joe, and Tim got hit by the rock, Tim can still sue Mike because Mike intended the throwing of the rock and the throwing of the rock caused the injury. The plaintiff must also prove that the intentional action was the proximate or direct cause of the injury, and the victim was damaged or injured in some way for which the law provides recovery.

PROVING NEGLIGENT TORTS

To prove a negligent tort, the plaintiff must prove that the defendant's actions breached the reasonable standard of care. In other words, the plaintiff must prove that a reasonable person would have been more cautious and careful than the defendant in the case. He must prove that the defendant's negligent or careless behavior was the proximate or direct cause of the injury. Finally, the plaintiff must prove that he was actually injured and suffered damages and is entitled to be financially compensated for those damages.

Proximate Cause

Proximate cause means direct cause. It is used in tort law to determine whether a person is responsible for an injury that resulted from his actions. For example, if a person throws a bag of firecrackers on the floor and the blast causes a clock to fall on the head of the plaintiff, then it must be determined whether the throwing of the firecrackers was the proximate cause of the plaintiff's injury. If the plaintiff can prove that the clock fell because of the blast from the fireworks, then the plaintiff can likely recover damages since the action was the proximate cause of his injury.

Res Ipsa Loquitor

Res ipsa loquitor means the thing speaks for itself. It is used in tort cases as a standard of proof in which the plaintiff does not have to directly prove negligence. The doctrine of *res ipsa loquitor* essentially means that in some situations it is clear that the injury would not have occurred if the defendant had not been negligent or careless. Therefore, the facts of the case alone are sufficient to prove breach of reasonable duty of care and the plaintiff does not then have to provide any independent evidence of the breach of the reasonable duty of care.

Duty of Care

Duty of care is the legal standard to which a person is held. All citizens of the United States are expected to behave with reasonable care towards other citizens. This means they must not be so careless or negligent that they accidentally cause harm. The duty of care imposed is a reasonable person standard. Each person's actions are thus judged against how a hypothetical reasonable person would have behaved in the given situation. If a hypothetical reasonable person would have acted more carefully, as viewed in the eyes of the judge or jury deciding the case, then a person can be held to have breached a reasonable standard of care and can be sued for negligence.

Duty to Aid

In general within the United States, there is no duty to aid. This means if you see someone drowning and you do not throw them a life preserver, you usually cannot be held legally liable if he drowns. Exceptions exist in two situations: if you create the hazard or if a special relationship exists. If, for example, you throw a person overboard or send someone out in a sinking ship, you have created the hazard that put him in peril and you have a duty to aid lest you be found legally liable for his drowning and subject to a wrongful death lawsuit. A special relationship is the other exception. A special relationship exists for emergency workers or personnel, such as police or firefighters, who have a duty to aid. Parents also have a special relationship and duty to aid their minor children, as do employers to employees, property owners to invitees, and spouses to each other.

Damages

In tort cases, damages are designed to make the plaintiff whole or restore him to the situation he would have been in if the accident had not occurred. Common damages include medical bills, lost wages, pain and suffering, emotional distress, loss of consortium (which is loss of the companionship of the injured person), wrongful death damages (if the victim dies), and punitive damages (designed to punish the person who caused the injury). Damages are awarded by a judge or jury on the basis of the facts of each case and on the basis of the actual cost of losses sustained by the plaintiff.

Punitive Damages

Punitive damages are designed to act as a deterrent by punishing bad behavior. Punitive damages are not directly designed to compensate the plaintiff for his injuries or losses, although the punitive damages are paid to the plaintiff. Punitive damages are awarded when the defendant in a case acted egregiously, such as acting so recklessly that injury was almost sure to follow or acting in such a manner as to intentionally cause harm. Fear of punitive damages is designed to encourage people not to behave in a very dangerous manner and not to commit intentional wrongs or injuries.

Limitations: Punitive damages are imposed in certain cases if the jury awards a punitive damage verdict that is many times higher than the compensatory damages in a case. In some states, punitive damages are also limited in cases of medical malpractice as part of tort reform efforts, in order to lower the cost of medical malpractice insurance, and to keep health care costs lower for consumers as a whole. Limits are placed on punitive damages in order to protect defendants' rights and to avoid an abusive system in which plaintiffs benefit more than is reasonably fair in light of the nature and circumstances of their injury. Excessive damages typically result from an emotional reaction on the part of the jury who awarded the punitive damages.

Compensatory Damages

Compensatory damages are designed to compensate the plaintiff for actual losses he suffered. Compensatory damages are separate and distinct from punitive damages that are designed to punish the defendant. Compensatory damages include medical bills that a plaintiff incurred as a result of the injury. Compensatory damages also include lost wages, money the plaintiff lost as a result of his injury causing him to miss work. The presence of health insurance usually has no effect on the award of compensatory damages, although an insurance company may go to court to obtain a damage settlement if the insurance company paid the money for medical bills and the plaintiff subsequently won a settlement.

Intentional Infliction and Negligent Infliction of Emotional Distress

Intentional infliction of emotional distress and negligent infliction of emotional distress are both types of damages that a person can recover from in tort. Intentional infliction of emotional distress occurs when a defendant did an action on purpose that was likely to cause someone stress. For example, if a person comes to someone's home and threatens him with a gun, this activity is likely to cause emotional distress. Since it was intentional, the individual could sue for intentional infliction of emotional distress. Negligent infliction of emotional distress, on the other hand, occurs when someone breaches his duty of care and behaves in a reckless manner which causes emotional distress. For example, if someone is driving drunk and hits someone with his car, the victim may suffer emotional distress as a result of being hit by the drunk driver.

Wrongful Death

Wrongful death is a type of tort damage that is appropriate when a defendant's negligent or intentional tort leads to the death of the victim. The victim himself cannot sue for injury, so his estate sues for wrongful death instead. The estate – whoever may legally sue on behalf of the deceased victim- must prove all of the elements that the victim would have had to prove. The estate must prove the defendant acted either intentionally or negligently, the defendant's actions led to the death, and damages resulted because of the death.

Damages in a wrongful death lawsuit are calculated by determining the life expectancy of the person who was killed and the wages that the person would have brought home if he had lived the normal life span. The relationship between the deceased person and the person bringing the lawsuit, as well as the way in which the deceased person lived his life (i.e. was he well liked), are also taken into consideration when determining the appropriate wrongful death damages. Because wages play the largest role in wrongful death damages, the death of a child may be less compensated for than the death of an adult.

LOSS OF CONSORTIUM

Loss of consortium is a type of tort damage that often accompanies a wrongful death suit. Loss of consortium involves damages suffered by the relative of a victim of a tort. It is essentially the loss of companionship that a person suffers as a result of a defendant's negligent or intentional action that led to injury or death. Loss of consortium is appropriate when a defendant either injures someone so badly that the person is no longer the same companion he once was (i.e. puts someone into a coma) or he kills someone. The family member of the injured or deceased person suffers a compensable wrong in the form of the loss of the relationship. In some states, loss of consortium is limited to spouses, while in other states loss of consortium suits can be brought by children, parents, or siblings.

WRONGFUL BIRTH

Wrongful birth is a type of malpractice lawsuit that occurs when a doctor fails to diagnose a severe birth defect or problem before a child is born. The crux of the argument is that a reasonable doctor would have made a diagnosis relating to the child and that the parent would have discontinued the pregnancy had the doctor made the appropriate diagnosis. The damages appropriate in a wrongful birth lawsuit are the damages that a parent incurs to care for the disabled child.

MALPRACTICE CASES

Medical and legal malpractice cases are generally a subset of tort litigation. A doctor or lawyer who fails to do his job adequately causes harm to a plaintiff. The plaintiff can thus sue him in a civil lawsuit to recover for the actual damages the plaintiff incurred as a result of the professional's lack of skill. Generally, doctors and lawyers are both held to a reasonable professional standard. This means a lawyer will be judged on the basis of what a reasonable lawyer would have done, while a doctor will be charged on the basis of what a reasonable doctor would have done. Both lawyers and doctors carry malpractice insurance to protect them from lawsuits related to malpractice.

LIMITATIONS

Within the context of medical malpractice, many states place limits on the amount of non-compensatory damages. In other words, while a plaintiff is still legally entitled to recover under the law for any actual damages such as medical bills and lost wages that result from medical malpractice, the payment a plaintiff can receive for pain and suffering and for punitive damages to punish the doctor for his malpractice are limited and capped. These efforts are part of tort reform, a political principle which suggests that unreasonably high malpractice verdicts awarded by juries can lead to a rise in overall health care costs as a result of doctors' need to pay extremely high premiums for medical malpractice insurance. Limiting recovery for non-economic damages reduces the potential risk of liability which reduces insurance costs and thus reducing health care costs.

PROVING MEDICAL MALPRACTICE

The plaintiff in a malpractice case must prove that the professional- whether a doctor or lawyer- breached the standard of care that a reasonable doctor or lawyer would have used in the given situation. The plaintiff must also prove that this breach was the direct or proximate cause of an injury. For example, if someone has a heart attack because a doctor misdiagnosed him, he must prove that a reasonable doctor would have correctly diagnosed him and that the heart attack and the resulting damage resulted from the misdiagnosis. Finally, the plaintiff must prove that he suffered actual damages.

SOURCES OF TORT LAW

The vast majority of tort law comes from common law. This means that the body of tort law is found in legal cases and opinions by judges, as opposed to statutes passed by the legislature. Tort law and the common law tort rules in the United States date back to the roots of the legal system in England. Tort law may differ slightly on a state-by-state basis and, while the Restatement of Torts summarizes majority and minority views on tort issues, citizens generally must turn to case law within each own state to understand the tort rules that will apply.

CONTRIBUTORY AND COMPARATIVE NEGLIGENCE

Contributory and comparative negligence are both defenses to a tort lawsuit. Contributory and comparative negligence both apply when a plaintiff is partially at fault for an accident. In other words, the direct or proximate cause of the action is both the negligence or carelessness on the part of the plaintiff and the negligence or carelessness on the part of the defendant. It is the burden of the defendant to prove either contributory or comparative negligence, as both are defenses that will reduce his legal obligation for damages to the plaintiff.

Contributory negligence bars recovery if the plaintiff was in part responsible for his own injuries. Comparative negligence allows the plaintiff to recover, but reduces that recovery based upon the percentage of responsibility that belongs to the plaintiff. For example, if a plaintiff walked out into the middle of the road without looking and was then hit by a driver who was not paying attention, both the plaintiff and driver are partially responsible for the plaintiff's injuries Under contributory negligence, the plaintiff would not have been able to recover. Most states have now adopted comparative negligence, which will allow the plaintiff to partially recover. A jury determines what percentage of the fault belongs to the plaintiff and reduces the recovery by that percentage.

REASONABLE PERSON STANDARD

The reasonable person standard says that everyone has the obligation to behave with a reasonable duty of care. The hypothetical reasonable person is the same regardless of who the defendant is, except in cases of professional malpractice or cases where children are involved. In other words, intelligence, age, and education level are not taken into consideration when determining whether a defendant in a tort action behaved with the degree of care with which a reasonable person would have behaved. The judge or jury in the case evaluates the defendant's behavior in light of the hypothetical reasonable person.

ALTERNATE TORT STANDARDS

A general reasonable person standard is not used in a case where a child has committed a tort or in professional malpractice cases. If a child commits a tort, that child's liability and duty of care is determined by looking at a reasonable child of the same age. For example, a four-year-old is held to the standard of care that a reasonable four-year-old would have exhibited, while a fourteen-year-old is held to the standard of care that a reasonable fourteen-year -old would have exhibited. The other exception occurs when a doctor or lawyer is sued for medical malpractice. The doctor is held to a reasonable doctor standard and the lawyer to a reasonable lawyer standard.

EGGSHELL PLAINTIFF

The eggshell plaintiff doctrine essentially means that, in tort cases, you take the plaintiff as you found him. If, for example, a plaintiff is especially susceptible to injury or to breaking a bone, you are still responsible for breaking that bone if you were negligent or intentionally injured the plaintiff. It does not matter if you intended the extent of the harm or if the plaintiff was injured far more than any other normal plaintiff would have been; the defendant is still responsible for any and all injury caused to the plaintiff by his negligent or intentional actions that caused harm.

Vicarious Liability

In certain cases, parents can be held liable for the torts of their children under the doctrine of vicarious liability. Generally, the law requires that the parent have had an indication that the child was likely to commit a tort, or that the parent was negligent in supervising the child. Employers can also be held vicariously liable for the torts committed by their employees provided the tort was committed in the line of work and was not a violation of express company policy.

Strict Liability and General Tort Cases

In most tort cases, the plaintiff must prove either negligence or an intentional action. In other words, the plaintiff must prove that the defendant breached a duty of care and failed to act with the level of care that a reasonable person would have exhibited. In strict liability cases, the plaintiff does not have to prove either negligence or intent. He simply has to prove that injury occurred and that he was damaged. Strict liability applies in certain cases, such as product liability.

Strict liability applies in several situations. Strict liability exists in most states in product liability law. This means that a manufacturer of a product or a seller of a product can be held strictly liable even if the manufacturer or seller was not negligent. Strict liability may also apply in certain states when it comes to dog bites; an owner may be held strictly liable if his dog bites someone, even if there has been no sign or indication to suggest the dog would bite.

Insurance

Most businesses and individuals purchase insurance in order to protect themselves from the financial risk of tort liability. In fact, every state in the United States requires that all drivers purchase liability insurance to protect themselves from the financial loss associated with causing a car accident. This legal rule is in place to ensure that victims of a car accident receive appropriate compensation and that the cost of their medical care is not passed on to the state. Homeowners insurance and business liability insurance are other examples of insurance designed to protect against liability and are generally purchased on a voluntary basis (although if a home has a mortgage against it, the lender may require homeowners insurance).

Protection Against Tort Liability Exposure

A person can protect himself from being sued in torts by acting with a reasonable duty of care and by not committing intentional actions designed to cause injury. A person can also protect himself from accidentally causing injury by purchasing the appropriate types of liability insurance. A person should ensure he has sufficient insurance to protect all of his assets and that the liability limit on insurance policies is high enough that it will not quickly be exhausted if he is sued for causing injury or damage.

Standard of Proof

In a tort law case, the standard of proof is "preponderance of the evidence." This means that the plaintiff and his attorney must convince the jury that *more likely than not* all of the evidence points to the fact that the defendant was negligent, that the negligence caused the injury, and that the plaintiff was actually damaged. This standard of proof is a less stringent standard than the *beyond a reasonable doubt* standard found in criminal law cases. The defendant, on the other hand, has the burden of proof when it comes to defenses against torts, such as self-defense or contributory or comparative negligence.

Contingent Fee Agreements

Many lawyers charge on a contingent fee basis for tort cases. This means that instead of being charged an hourly fee, clients pay a percentage of the amount they recover in damages. This allows a plaintiff who doesn't have the money or who does not wish to pay legal bills to still sue the tortfeasor who caused the injury. In this way, it encourages accountability on the part of tortfeasors who know they may be subject to a negligence lawsuit. Contingent fee arrangements are thus permitted by the law in tort or civil suits, although they are forbidden in divorce cases and criminal cases as a matter of public policy.

CLASS ACTIONS

Class action lawsuits occur when a number of plaintiffs suffered a similar injury or wrong at the hands of one defendant. This commonly occurs in product liability cases where hundreds of millions of people may have been injured by a defective drug or product. It allows each plaintiff to recover even when the damages were relatively minor, since the plaintiff does not have to bring his own legal suit. In this way, class action lawsuits also help to ensure that defendants will be held accountable. Class actions also result in less of a backlog of cases on a court docket, since many cases relating to one particular incident will all be addressed in one class action tort case.

Miscellaneous

Agency

As it relates to the conduct of business, the concept of agency may be defined as the legal relationship between two parties in which one party (the agent) represents the other party (the principal) and is authorized to perform certain acts for and on behalf of the principal. The principal is bound by the acts of the agent, which the agent performs in carrying out entrusted duties within the scope of the agent's authority. Consider what would happen without the concept of agency: no one would be able to employ or enlist a representative to perform his desired functions, and instead would be limited to only acting directly for himself. Further, since corporations are by definition incapable of performing these functions, in the absence of agency law corporations would cease to function.

Employment and Power of Attorney

Agency may or may not include employment, depending on the definition of "employment." If an agent is deemed to be under the direct control and supervision of the hiring party, and this party determines both the work the agent is to perform and the manner in which he is to perform it, then the agent is considered an employee of the party in question.

Note that the 1959 Restatement of Agency considers the above-mentioned restriction as being too narrow, instead asserting that employees are always agents. This is not, however, a universally-held view -- some courts and observers have asserted that certain types of employees do not have the power to represent the employer and therefore cannot be considered agents of that employer.

As to the relationship between agency and power of attorney, agency includes and may be created by a power of attorney.

Independent Contractor

An independent contractor may be defined as a person who is hired to do a piece of work according to contractually-defined conditions and without being subject to control except as to the result of the work. It is the purview of the independent contractor to determine what tools and techniques he chooses to use. Whereas an employee often acts as an agent of the employer, an independent contractor rarely functions as such an agent. Independent contractors create fewer administrative burdens for an employer and can save an employer the significant expenses of paying social security tax, unemployment tax, and the expenses arising from benefits such as health insurance.

Some of the factors to be considered when applying the "economic realities" test to determine if someone is an employee or an independent contractor include:

- Degree of skill -- Contractors are expected to require no training.
- Level of supervision -- Contractors are expected to require little supervision.
- Source of tools and materials -- Contractors usually provide their own tools and materials.
- Whether the work is part of the hirer's regular business
- Opportunity for profits or losses
- Payment calculation method (e.g., payment for time worked vs. payment by the job)
- Permanency of the work relationship -- Long-term implies employment.
- Provision of benefits (e.g., sick leave, retirement benefits) – Benefits are not typically offered to contractors.
- The parties' written intent

Personal Service Obligations

In short, an agent cannot be called upon to perform personal service obligations. This is because these obligations usually require the services of a designated person in possession of special skills or judgment to do the job, and one who cannot send a representative to act in his behalf. An example may be when a business owner assigns an employee a specific task related to the functioning of the business. When the business owner sells the business to a third party, this third party cannot claim the services of the employee. By contrast, those tasks that may be delegated to an agent or subagent are generally ones not requiring the delegating party's special skills or judgment.

Creating Relationships of Agency

The principle methods that can create relationships of agency are:

- By express contract or by consensual agreement -- The agency relationship is usually created by an oral or written contract. In the absence of contract, however, either party may terminate the relationship at any time without liability to the other party.
- By the conduct of the parties -- a.k.a. implied contracts of agency. Agency is deemed to exist by nature of the parties' actions, which would tend to lead others to believe an agency existed.
- By ratification of an unauthorized act -- an implied contract that occurs after an "agent" performs a valid act ostensibly on behalf of the principal
- By estoppel -- The "agent" acquires apparent authority when by the nature of his actions on behalf of the principal he leads another to reasonably believe the agent is indeed authorized.
- By necessity -- occurring in those special circumstances in which one person is responsible for the necessities of another (e.g., a parent's responsibility to a child)

Fiduciary

A fiduciary is a person legally appointed and authorized to hold assets in trust for another person. The fiduciary manages the assets for the benefit of the other person, and, unlike people in ordinary business relationships, a fiduciary may not seek to attain personal benefit from their transactions with those he represents. One of the main obligations of a fiduciary is to fully account for moneys collected for his principal. A fiduciary is prohibited from commingling such monies with the fiduciary's own monies and may not appropriate the principal's property for his own use.

Agent Duties

The duties required of an agent include:

- Duty to obey instructions -- Beyond the self-evident nature of this duty, an agent is forbidden from entering the principal into unauthorized contracts, from improperly delegating his duties, or from committing torts that may accrue to his principal.
- Duty to act with skill -- Failure of the agent to perform up to the proper standard of care and skill will constitute a breach of contract.
- Duty to avoid conflict of interest -- An agent is prohibited from acting in his own self-interest when carrying out his responsibilities to his principal.
- Duty to protect confidential information

- Duty to notify -- The agent must notify the principal of all information that may be useful to the principal in matters relevant to his employ.
- Duty to account -- The agent must maintain an "open book," by which the principal can evaluate the progress of the work.

Duties of a Principal

The principal's primary duty is to compensate the agent for his services in accordance to the terms of the agency contract. In the event of an implied contract, the principal is obliged to compensate the agent by means of the agent's fee as it is understood by both parties or as it is generally understood. In the absence of either an actual or an implied contract, the agent is entitled to reasonable compensation for the services performed. The principal is responsible to compensate the agent for all reasonable expenses incurred by the agent in pursuit of the principal's business. The principal also must inform the agent of any risks of which the principal is aware.

Actual Authority and Apparent Authority

First, note that the legal meaning of authority is the power to act granted by a principal to his or her agent. Actual authority is defined as the authority that a principal, in reality, has granted to an agent. Actual authority can be one of either (a) express authority in which explicit oral or written words are conveyed by the principal to the agent; or (b) implied authority in which authority may be inferred from the words or actions conveyed by the principal to the agent. Apparent authority is characterized by a principal purposely (or through negligence) leading a third party to believe that the principal's agent has actual authority, although such authority has not in reality been granted. Note that a principal is legally bound by the acts of an agent acting with apparent authority.

Direct Liability

Direct liability may be defined as the legal obligation of a principal because of negligent acts. The concept of direct liability renders a principal directly responsibility for his agent's torts if any of the following conditions occurs:

- Improper orders or instructions given by the principal to his agent resulted in the agent's tort.
- The principal chose or employed his agent in an improper or negligent manner.
- The principal had a responsibility to properly supervise or oversee the agent, but failed to do so.

Indirect Liability and Tests for Respondeat Superior

Indirect liability occurs when an agent's negligence in acting for the principal in the scope of his employment (i.e., Respondeat Superior) is charged to the principal, even though the principal has committed no act of negligence himself. The tests for Respondeat Superior are:

- The agent's conduct must be the type of conduct that the principal hired the agent to perform.
- The agent's conduct must occur in the ordinary course of the agent performing his assigned duties, that is, at the authorized place and time of employment.
- The agent's conduct must not be in service of the agent's self-interest, but must occur in service to the principal.
- The principal could have anticipated the conduct exhibited by the agent.

Disclosed Principal

A disclosed principal is a principal whose identity is shared by his or her agent with a third party. The fact of the agency and the identity of the principal are typically disclosed in any contract with the third party. If an agent negotiates a contract between a principal and a third party and signs the name of the principal, he must employ wording indicating that he is acting in his capacity as the principal's agent, e.g., "by," "for" or "agent for." In so doing, the agent indicates his capacity as a representative and consequently binds the principal, not himself. If, however, the agent in fact has no authority, but merely claims to represent the principal even if the principal is disclosed, the agent may have personal liability. Further, in the event that the agent frequently acts for or appears to have the authority of the principal, but the principal has not actually given or has withdrawn that authority, both the principal and the agent may be liable to the third party.

Partially Disclosed Principal and Undisclosed Principal

The concept of a partially disclosed principal arises when a principal seeks privacy or otherwise desires to conceal his identity, his identity thus remaining unknown to a third party in his dealings with the principal's agent. In this case, the agent is liable on the contract. Note, however, that the principal may also be deemed liable on the contract in the event that the principal is identified and the agent cannot satisfy the contract.

The concept of an undisclosed principal arises when the third party knows neither the identity of the principal nor the agency relationship between the agent and the principal. In this case, the third party has no reason to believe that the agent is acting in an agency relationship with the principal, therefore rendering the agent liable on the contract.

Tort Liability of Agents

Regardless of whether or not an agent is acting within the scope of his employment, an agent who commits a tort is personally liable for the tort. If the commission of the tort occurred in the normal scope of the agent's employment, then the principal is also liable for the tort. In these latter cases, an injured third party may seek damages from either the principal or the agent, or both (but not a double recovery). If a crime committed by an agent has occurred under the direction, approval, or with the participation of the principal, both the agent and the principal are criminally liable. If an employer knows, or should have known, that his employee is committing criminal acts in the course of his employment, the employer may himself be criminally liable, and an employer may be liable if he fails to adequately supervise or delegate work to an employee who violates criminal laws.

Termination of Agency Relation

The ways that an agency relation may be terminated are as follows:

- Death or incapacity of either the principal or the agent
- Bankruptcy of either the principal or the agent
- Irresolvable impediments to the purpose of the agency (e.g., damage or loss to goods, changes to business conditions, etc.
- The business enterprise itself proves to contravene jurisdictional laws.
- Either the principal or the agent proves to be irreversibly incapable of performing his duties.
- Actions of either the principal or the agent constitute a material breach of the contract.

Business Organizations

Three types of business organizations are:

1. Sole proprietorship -- the simplest type of business organization, in which the sole owner and the business are legally considered to be identical entities. Thus, debts of the business are the legal responsibility of the sole owner.
2. Partnership -- Two or more individuals agree to form and operate for profit a business, of which they are the owners. There are two types of partnership: general and limited.
3. Corporation -- a distinct legal entity typically created under state law, whose existence is separate and distinct from its shareholder owners. In order to be deemed a corporation for tax purposes, a corporation must exhibit three of the following four characteristics: (1) limited liability; (2) centralized management; (3) continuity of life; and (4) free transferability of interests.

General Partnership

Creating a Partnership

A partnership agreement is all that is required to create a partnership; no special formalities are necessary. This agreement can be express or implied though from a practical standpoint it is preferable to be in the form of a written document. In the absence of such a written document there is a greater likelihood that, in the case of disputes among partners, such disputes are more likely to be difficult to settle.

Rights and Duties of Partners

As per the Uniform Partnership Act, the primary duty of partners in a general partnership is to carry on the business of the partnership in a manner that confers upon the partnership the greatest common advantage. Unless otherwise codified in the partnership agreement, each partner has one vote, and ordinary business decisions are decided by majority vote.

Decisions Requiring Unanimous Consent

The types of decisions that generally require unanimous consent of all the partners include:

- Amending the partnership agreement
- Changing the nature of the partnership's business
- Making modifications to the partnership's capital structure
- Conveying or mortgaging property or serving as a surety or guarantor (unless these are in the partnership's customary line of business)
- Any act that may not readily be discerned as representing the business's ordinary way of operating
- Confessing judgment or submitting to arbitration

Rules

Some of the important rules for partnerships promulgated by the Uniform Partnership Act include:

- Partners must work on behalf of the partnership
- Partners are entitled to profits, but not to being paid a salary
- Partners may examine the partnership's records and are entitled to an accounting of the partnership's assets

- A partner must maintain confidentiality and must inform all other partners of communications sent to him
- Each partner has a property interest in the partnership and is a tenant in partnership of all partnership property

Binding the Entire General Partnership to the Actions of a Single Partner

The four means by which a third party can bind the entire general partnership to the actions of a single partner are:

1. Apparent authority -- Similar to the agency concept of apparent authority but broader in nature, due to the fact that the partner is not simply an agent or employee but is in fact an owner or principal. Apparent authority is dependent on the third party's reasonable belief in the partner's authority.
2. Express actual authority -- arising directly from the formal partnership agreement
3. Implied actual authority -- arising from the nature of the partnership's business and/or the law of partnerships
4. Ratification by the other partners after the individual partner's acts

Termination Through Dissolution by Acts of the Parties

A general partnership can be terminated through dissolution by acts of the parties in any of the following manners:

- The partners agree to dissolve the partnership.
- Either the partnership's term of duration expires or the purpose for which the partnership was created has been accomplished. Both of these eventualities are typically codified in the partnership agreement.
- Except in the case in which the partnership agreement precludes it, a partner is expelled or withdraws of his own volition from the partnership. Note that departing partners remain liable for partnership obligations that existed prior to their departure.

Dissolution

The dissolution of a general partnership is accomplished (a) through operation of the law in any of the following manners:

- Illegality -- The situation arises whereby it would be against the law to continue the partnership or to conduct the partnership's business with one or more of the partners.
- Bankruptcy -- of either the partnership itself or of one or more of the partners
- In the event of a partner's death

The dissolution is accomplished (b) through court decree in any of the following manners:

- A partner is rendered by reason of mental incapacity incapable of participating in management.
- A partner has breached the partnership agreement or has committed acts detrimental to the partnership.
- The business engaged in by the partnership can be operated only at a loss.
- Personal conflicts or other similar circumstances

Upon the dissolution of a general partnership, the following actions occur:

1. Liquidation -- also termed "winding up"; the dissolved partnership liquidation involves the sale of partnership assets, either paying or otherwise settling the debts incurred by the partnership, and compensating each partner in accordance with the value of his interest in the partnership
2. Distribution of assets -- occurring in the following order:
    a. Payment to creditors
    b. Paying off loans to the partnership made by a partner
    c. Return of each partner's investment
    d. Distribution of the remainder, according to the terms stated in the partnership agreement

Express Partnership Agreement

Some of the subjects commonly covered in a typical express partnership agreement include:

- Partnership name and type of business
- Duration of the agreement and conditions for closing out the business
- Identity of the partners and their expected contributions to the business
- Division of profits and losses
- Authority of the partners
- Procedures for amending the partnership agreement and for the addition or withdrawal of partners from the enterprise
- Accounting methods
- Form of management and the management of employees
- Arbitration of disputes

Implied Partnership

The three considerations that if satisfied would probably result in a court deeming a business relationship to be an implied partnership are:

1. Joint ownership of the business among the parties
2. Sharing of profits or losses among the parties
3. The parties possess equal management rights

Note that all three factors must be in evidence. For example, if two parties own an enterprise together and receive revenue from the enterprise's business, this is not sufficient in and of itself to constitute a partnership.

Partnership by Estoppel

Partnership by estoppel (also called presumption of partnership) is a legally binding partnership that occurs when a person misrepresents or causes another person to incorrectly conclude that the person making the misrepresentation is a partner, when in fact no formal partnership is in effect. Regardless of whether the alleged partnership is a fictitious or a real partnership, this misrepresentation will result in a judgment of partnership by estoppel. In either event, the alleged partner is legally liable to the other person for the credit or loans obtained by the partnership by estoppel on the basis of such misrepresentation.

Limited Partnership

A limited partnership (LP) is similar to a general partnership, except that in addition to the general partner(s) there are one or more limited partners who invest in the company and receive a specified share of the LP's profits, but are neither involved in management of the company nor liable for losses beyond the amount of their capital investment. A general partner in an LP has essentially the same rights and duties as partners in a general partnership, and as such are responsible for managing the entity and have unlimited personal liability for its debts. A limited partnership must conform to state statutory requirements, including filing of an LP certificate.

LP Certificate

The required information that must be present on an LP certificate includes:

- Partnership name and location
- Names and addresses of the partnership's agents, the partnership's general partners, and the partnership's limited partners
- Term of duration of the partnership
- Description of the LP's business
- Value of each partner's financial and material contributions to the partnership
- Enumeration of the partners' rights
- Description of the method by which the partnership can change partners and continue the business

Requirements

The requirements of a limited partner, any of which if violated may subject the limited partner to the same liability as a general partner, are:

- The LP's capital contribution must be in the form of money, property, services, a promissory note, or some other obligation such as a commitment to perform specified services.
- The limited partner's last name must not appear in the partnership name, which must include the exact phrase "limited partnership".
- The limited partner may not represent himself to be anything other than a limited partner.
- If the limited partner learns that the partnership certificate contains any false information, he must withdraw from the LP.

Corporation

A corporation may be defined as an artificial business entity that is chartered by a state and given a number of legal rights as an entity separate from its shareholders, directors, officers, and employees. A corporation is characterized by its existence as a going concern -- that is, if all the owners of the corporation were to vanish into thin air, the corporation would continue to exist as an entity owned by the heirs of the now-vanished previous owners. A corporation is also characterized by its issuance of shares of easily transferrable stock and the limited liability of its owners, who have separate legal standing from the corporation, protecting them from personal liability in the event the corporation is sued.

For most legal purposes, a corporation is treated in the identical manner as a living person. That is, the corporation can sue and be sued, can enter into contracts, can own property, and can be charged with criminal misconduct.

Piercing the Corporate Veil

The phrase "piercing the corporate veil" describes a situation in which the customary legal protections offered a principal in a corporation are set aside, leaving the principal personally liable for the corporation's debts. Specifically, the corporate veil may be pierced when the following two conditions exist: (1) the corporation is itself a guise, disguising a fraudulent purpose; and (2) the corporation operates in a manner inconsistent with the legal definition of a corporation. Some of the factors courts consider when deciding whether to pierce the corporate veil include:

- Commingling of the corporation's funds
- The absence of customary corporate formalities or structures
- Overlap in ownership
- Insufficient barriers between the corporation and its owners
- Insufficient barriers between the corporation and its subsidiaries

Owners and Businesses Being Separate Legal Entities

In the case of a sole proprietorship the owners and business are not separate legal entities.

Similarly, with partnerships, the owners and business are generally not separate legal entities, except for some purposes such as owning property in the business's name. On the other hand, with an LLC, the owners and business are separate legal entities. The owners and business are almost always separate legal entities in the case of corporations.

Corporations

De Jure and De Facto Corporations

The term de jure has the connotation of "as a matter of law." Thus, a de jure corporation is one that has been formed in accordance with the statutory formalities imposed by state corporation law in order to be granted corporate existence. The term de facto has the connotation of "as a matter of practice not founded on law". Thus, a de facto corporation is one that, due to failure to comply with some technical requirements, has not been properly formed, despite the good faith efforts of the creating parties to do so. Even though the corporation is thus imperfectly created, it is nevertheless treated as a corporation, shielding its shareholders from liability.

Public, Private, Quasi-Public Corporations

A public corporation is a corporation that is formed to meet a government or public purpose. An example might be a public transport company. Private corporations are created for private purposes, typically for the financial benefit of the officers and/or shareholders. Most corporations are private ones. A quasi-public corporation is a type of corporation that may be termed a "hybrid," in that it has features of both public and private corporations. A quasi-public corporation is a public utility, that is, a privately-owned business created for public purposes whose services and rates are strictly controlled.

Domestic, Foreign, and Alien Corporations

A domestic corporation is a US corporation that operates in the state in which it is incorporated (the opposite of a foreign corporation). A foreign corporation, in the US, is a corporation registered to do business in a state or jurisdiction differing from the one in which it was incorporated; alternately, it is a corporation incorporated in a foreign country that is authorized to do business in the US An alien corporation is a company incorporated in a foreign country and is occasionally used as a synonym for foreign corporation, but in the US the term foreign corporation denotes doing business in a state or jurisdiction other than the one in which it was incorporated.

Federal, Nonprofit, and Membership Corporation

A federal corporation is a type of corporation created by the government for strictly defined purposes, such as the system of national banks and savings and loans. Nonprofit corporations are corporations created to serve a purpose other than the generation of profits for distribution among stockholders. A nonprofit corporation has no shareholders, but does have a board of directors and officers who may not receive a distribution of (any money from) profits. Membership corporation is another term for a nonprofit corporation that is created to serve a purpose other than the generation of profits for distribution among stockholders; examples include religious societies and trade unions.

Unlimited Liability and Limited Liability

Under unlimited liability, the losses incurred by the business result in personal losses by the business owner. Any debts or damages incurred by the business become the personal debts and damages that are the responsibility the business owner to ameliorate, whether by selling off assets such as bank accounts, real estate (possibly including the business owner's home) or personal property, such as jewelry or automobiles. Also, under unlimited liability, each partner is responsible for the business's losses, no matter if these losses were caused by one of the business's partners.

Under limited liability, the partners are not responsible for debts or losses incurred by the company above and beyond the value of their investment in the business. Here, personal assets may not be seized to compensate creditors.

Rights Entitled to Shareholders

The rights to which a corporation's shareholders are entitled include:

- The right to approve gifts -- including gifts to charities, bonuses, stock options, and incentive plans not contractually defined
- The right of inspection -- Within certain limits, shareholders are entitled to examine the corporation's books, including annual reports, minutes of meetings, corporate bylaws, and lists of shareholders.
- The right to share in dividends -- The board of directors decides how dividends are to be distributed. Absent an agreement to the contrary, all holders of a particular class of stock have identical rights regarding the disbursement of dividends.
- Preemptive rights -- the right of existing shareholders to preempt the sale of subsequent stock to new purchasers in order to maintain the existing shareholders' percentage interest in the corporation

Lawsuits Brought by Shareholders

Derivative lawsuits are brought by shareholders in the interest of the corporation, often against individual officers or directors for reasons of waste or for conflict of interest. In the event of a successful lawsuit, the shareholders themselves do not profit, and any recovery belongs to the corporation (including attorney fees, if applicable). In the event of an unsuccessful shareholders' lawsuit, the shareholders may be responsible to reimburse the defendant for his expenses (including attorney fees, if applicable). By contrast, individual lawsuits are those legal actions brought by an individual shareholder against the corporation in order to shield the individual's personal rights or property in the business.

Board of directors and officers

Fiduciary Responsibilities

The four most important fiduciary responsibilities of a corporate board of directors and the corporate officers are:

1. Duty of loyalty -- Both the directors and officers owe unreserved loyalty to the corporation and its shareholders. Managers may not conceal or fail to disclose any personal interest they may have in any matter involving the corporation or its business and must recuse themselves from taking any action in relation to such matters.
2. No usurpation of corporate opportunity -- Neither directors or officers may personally engage in any business opportunity that could otherwise have been a business opportunity for the corporation.
3. Corporate officers are forbidden to utilize corporate assets for their personal use.
4. Restrictions on transactions in shares -- Corporate officers may not receive stock on terms advantageous to themselves but not to other shareholders.

Standards in Compliance with the Business Judgment Rule

Those standards that corporate directors and officers must uphold to be in compliance with the Business Judgment Rule are:

- Exercise of due care -- This includes making informed decisions and taking into consideration all the factors that might be reasonably assumed to bear upon the issue at hand.
- Action in good faith -- Officers and directors are immune from liability to the corporation for losses incurred in corporate transactions within their authority, so long as the transactions are made in good faith and with reasonable skill and prudence. Inaction is protected only when it arises from a conscious decision, as opposed to a simple failure to act.
- Reasonable belief that the action is in the best corporate interest -- Unwise business decisions or honest errors in judgment are generally matters that are of no consequence in a court of law. Mistakes or errors in the exercise of honest business judgment do not subject the officers and directors to liability for negligence in the discharge of their appointed duties.

Corporate Officers

The following is a list of and the roles of corporate officers:

- President -- the chief executive officer (CEO) of the corporation. The president may be on the corporation's board of directors, and he may preside at board and/or shareholder meetings.
- Vice president -- assumes the responsibilities of the president when the president is absent; the VP is also responsible to supervise various line activities, such as sales, accounting, and administration.
- Secretary -- Generally in charge of no executive functions, the secretary is in charge of the corporate books and records. In large firms, the secretary is often an attorney.
- Treasurer -- Generally in charge of no executive functions, the treasurer is responsible for management of the firm's funds.

DIVIDEND AND DISTRIBUTION

A dividend is the distribution in cash or stock of a corporation's earnings to its shareholders. By contrast, a distribution refers to the distribution of a corporation's assets (stock not being considered a corporate asset).

- Decision to declare a dividend -- the prerogative of the board of directors, not subject to shareholders' desires
- Form of dividend -- may be in the form of cash, shares of stock, real estate, or other tangibles
- Restrictions on dividends -- Creditors may restrict the corporation's ability to pay dividends.
- Effect of illegal dividend -- Any director who promulgates an illegal dividend will be held liable for that portion of the dividend arising from the illegality.

REGISTRATION STATEMENT AND STATUTORY PROSPECTUS

The registration statement is a detailed document filed by a corporation with the Securities and Exchange Commission prior to an initial public offering. The registration statement contains all relevant information about the security to be offered, the issuer and the business involved, and plans for the proceeds of the offering. The officers of the corporation (CEO, CFO, board of directors) are liable for errors in the statement.

The statutory prospectus is an informing -- not a promoting -- document that is regulated by federal law and must be furnished to an investor before a purchase is made. Information contained in the prospectus is culled from the registration statement and details all material facts relating to the company and its operations so that a prospective investor can make an informed decision as to the merit of the investment.

SECURITY ACT OF 1933 AND CIVIL LIABILITY

The five conditions under which the Security Act of 1933 provides for civil liability, as well as the remedy in each case are:

1. The sale of an unregistered security that was required to have been registered; Remedy: rescission of the transaction or damages
2. The sale of a registered security in the absence of a statutory prospectus; Remedy: rescission of the transaction or damages
3. The offering of a security sale prior to the filling or approval of a registration statement; Remedy: rescission of the transaction or damages
4. The presence of a false statement in the registration statement; Remedy: the price paid for the securities less the market price at the time of the lawsuit
5. The omission of a material fact from the registration statement; Remedy: the price paid for the securities less the market price at the time of the lawsuit

GOALS OF THE SECURITIES EXCHANGE ACT OF 1934

The four major goals of the Securities Exchange Act of 1934 are:

1. Regulation of the securities market and security exchanges; the Securities Exchange Act established the Securities and Exchange Commission with which all stock exchanges, over-the-counter brokers, and dealers must register. Recent legislation allows the SEC to regulate trading practices, impose fines, disbar defrauders, and even suspend trading during times of high volatility.

2. To provide persons who buy and sell securities with information concerning the issuers of such securities
3. To prevent securities fraud
4. To prevent the use of insider information in the trading of securities

Sarbanes–Oxley Act (SOX) of 2002

The Sarbanes–Oxley Act was enacted in 2002 as a response to a multitude of accounting and corporate scandals, the most notorious of which occurred at Enron, Adelphia, WorldCom, and Tyco International. These scandals cost investors billions of dollars when the offending companies' stock dropped precipitously, resulting in a major loss of investor confidence in the securities markets. The legislation, which does not apply to privately-held companies, provides new and enhanced standards and procedures for publicly- held companies, including more transparent financial disclosure and more accurate assessment of risk.

One of the key requirements SOX has placed upon corporations is Section 906(a), which mandates that the chief executive officer and the chief financial officer of the corporation personally certify that the financial statements included in the corporation's periodic report are fully compliant with all terms of the 1934 Securities Exchange Act, and that they accurately represent the corporation's financial condition. Another key requirement concerns the retention of corporate documents, specifying criminal liability for anyone who knowingly destroys documents relevant to a federal investigation or bankruptcy filing. SOX also holds a corporation's accountants criminally liable for their participation in securities fraud and prohibits most corporate loans to the corporation's senior executives.

"S" Corporation

The principal requirement of an "S" corporation is that it has no more than 100 shareholders. An "S" corporation must be a domestic corporation or a limited liability corporation, and it must have only one class of stock. Profits and losses for an "S" corporation must be allocated to shareholders proportionately to each one's interest in the business.

The main objective in establishing an "S" corporation is to avoid the so-called "double taxation" incurred by a "C" corporation, whereby the corporation's earnings are taxed first at the corporate level and then taxed again upon distribution to the shareholders. Instead, in an "S" corporation, the corporation's income or losses are divided among and passed through to its shareholders. The shareholders must then report the income or loss on their own individual income tax returns. This concept is called single taxation.

Articles of Incorporation Items

The items required in a corporation's articles of incorporation typically include:

- Names of the incorporators -- solely for the purpose of lending their names to the incorporating documents
- Corporation name -- The corporation's name must include one of these words abbreviated: Company, Corporation, Incorporated, or Limited.
- Corporate address and name and address of resident agent -- the person authorized to receive official papers
- Duration -- either perpetual or limited
- Purpose -- usually identifies the specific type of business, e.g., restaurant

- Capital structure -- generally, number and classes of shares of stock, as well as other matters relating to equity and capital
- Internal organization -- typically, the number of directors, names and addresses of interim board members, etc.

HANDLING PROFITS AND LOSSES

Profits and losses are handled as follows in the following types of business organization:

- Corporation -- After paying salaries to employees and officers, profits are retained by the corporation and/or distributed to stockholders as dividends.
- LLC -- generally shared equally by partners, unless otherwise specified in the partnership agreement
- Partnership -- generally shared equally by partners, unless otherwise specified in the partnership agreement
- Sole proprietorship -- Profits and losses belong solely to the proprietor.

BLUE SKY LAWS

"Blue sky laws" are laws on the books in every state in the union and are designed to protect investors against security fraud. Similar in scope and purpose to the Securities Act of 1933, blue sky laws require sellers of new stock issues or mutual funds to register their offerings and provide financial details on each issue so that investors can base their judgments on relevant data. The term is said to have originated with a judge who asserted that a particular stock offering had as much value as a patch of blue sky.

LIABILITY FOR ACCOUNTANTS AND FINANCIAL OFFICERS

Securities laws address liability for accountants and financial officers thus:

- Civil liability -- Issuers of new securities, in particular accountants and financial officers, may incur civil liability for misstatements or omissions of material fact in registration statements.
- Criminal liability -- The 1933 Securities Act provides penalties for any defendant, including a participating accountant, convicted of a criminal violation of securities law.
- Common law tort liability -- This refers to malpractice suits against professionals such as doctors, lawyers and accountants. The applicable standard of care is generally based upon testimony by other professionals in the field. For accountants, the standard applied is usually GAAP (generally accepted accounting standards) or GAAS (generally accepted auditing standards).

LLC

A Limited Liability Corporation (LLC) is a relatively recent type of US business structure that combines the limited personal liability feature of a corporation with the single taxation feature of a partnership or sole-proprietorship firm. Whereas "S" corporations are permitted to issue only one type of stock, an LLC has no such restrictions and may issue multiple classes of stock. While "S" corporations are not permitted to own subsidiaries, LLCs are so permitted. Additionally, LLCs have no restrictions on the type and number of owners. For federal tax purposes, an LLC is treated like a partnership, in that tax returns for an LLC are filed with the taxation authorities only for the purpose of information, with each shareholder separately filing his own tax return.

Disadvantages

While LLCs are not subject to federal income tax, they, unlike general partnerships, are sometimes subject to state income tax, which points out another drawback: there are no uniform laws governing LLCs and such laws varying widely from state to state, complicating the conduct of business across state lines. Another drawback to LLCs is that they are not considered perpetual entities, in contrast to corporations, which exist in perpetuity. Absent a clause in the Operating Agreement providing for the continuance of the LLC in the event of the death or withdrawal of a member, the LLC will cease to exist when such events occur. Finally, since LLCs are a relatively recent form of business organization, statutes governing LLCs are still evolving, and there is a dearth of case history to indicate how courts may interpret existing laws.

Advantages

First and foremost, an LLC confers upon its members (owners) limited liability protection from being personally responsible for the debt liabilities of the company -- members are only personally liable to the extent of their personal investment in the company. Should the business go bankrupt or should a court hold against an LLC, a member's personal assets remain out of legal reach. LLCs, like "S" corporations, are exempt from the so-called "double taxation" required of "C" corporations. The LLC's profits pass through the company and to the company's members, who report their individual profits on their federal tax returns (note that LLCs may have to pay state and local taxes). LLCs are not subject to the limitations on ownership to which "S" corporations are subject.

Management Structure of Corporations

The following types of corporations have management structures as delineated here:

- Partnership -- Unless otherwise stated in the partnership agreement, general partners have equal votes in the corporation. In a limited partnership, limited partners have no management rights.
- LLC -- Management structure is similar to that of a general partnership, whereby management is governed by decisions made in the partnership agreement.
- Sole proprietorship -- Management consists of the sole proprietor, himself.
- Corporation -- Management and owners are distinct and separate. Officers are appointed by directors, who are elected by stockholders on a pro rata basis depending on their number of shares.

Requirements for Creating Business Organizations

The basic requirements for creating the following types of business organizations are:

- Sole proprietorship -- The easiest to organize, a sole proprietorship is subject to few, if any, restrictions.
- Corporation -- created by statutory authorization; in order to receive a state charter, a would-be corporation must meet state requirements.
- Partnership -- created by either written or implied agreement of the partners, but must file a statutory form.
- LLC -- created by statutory authorization; as in the case of a corporation, an LLC must file articles of incorporation.

LLP

A Limited Liability Partnership (LLP) is quite similar to a general partnership and provides an individual partner protection against personal liability for certain partnership obligations. There is one important distinction, however: Whereas individual partners in a general partnership are liable for the partnership's debts and obligations, individual partners in an LLP are protected against personal liability for certain partnership liabilities. The first LLP statute, enacted in Texas in 1991, protected partners from personal liability for claims related to a co-partner's negligence, error, omission, incompetency, or malfeasance. Also, in the case of errors, omissions, incompetence or negligence on the part of the partnership's employees or other agents, the statute permanently limited the personal liability of the individual partners. Today, individual state laws vary in their scope as these laws relate to LLPs.

Advantages

The principal advantage of an LLP is that, as in an LLC, partners are offered limited personal liability from the debts of the partnership, each partner being liable only for the pro rata amount of his investment in the company. Thus, an LLP may be considered more secure and less financially risky than a partnership. Another advantage of an LLP is that, as in a general partnership, an LLP is exempt from the so-called "double taxation" required of "C" corporations. The LLP's profits pass through the company and to the company's members, who report their individual profits on their federal tax returns. Since an LLP's partners directly own and/or control the business, LLPs provide these partners with the ability to make executive decisions for the company without the burdens under which the operating officers of a corporation must operate.

Disadvantages

Not all states have similar laws regarding the liability of partners in a limited liability partnership. Some states limit liability only for negligent civil wrongdoings, but allow personal liability for intentional torts or criminal actions. Other states restrict liability, even for intentional torts, but there may be some situations where personal liability may arise. Another disadvantage of LLPs is that some states place restrictions on what professions may enter into a limited liability partnership. A further disadvantage of LLPs is that the partnership remains liable for the actions taken by a partner in the furtherance of the partnership's business, thus offering its partners less protection than that provided to shareholders in a corporation.

Important Terms

Attorney at law -- an attorney who practices law (as contrasted with patent agents or paralegals), and who is employed to represent a client in legal matters

Attorney in fact -- a person who is authorized under a power of attorney, a written document establishing the appointment, to represent another party; the appointment may be for broad or for specific purposes

Power of attorney -- the written legal authority given by one party (the principal) to another (the attorney in fact) to act on the principal's behalf

Debenture -- An unsecured corporate bond that does not have a line of income or a piece of property or equipment to guarantee repayment of principal upon maturity.

Callable bond -- a bond that can be redeemed by its issuer prior to maturity

Convertible bond -- a bond that can be converted into a specified amount of the corporation's equity at the discretion of the bondholder

Indenture -- a legal document detailing the terms and legal structure under which debt securities are issued

Equity securities -- a security issued by a corporation representing an ownership right in the corporation and a share of the corporation's profits

Distribution of dividends -- Holders of preferred shares may receive a share of dividends before common stockholders.

Distribution upon liquidation -- Upon the company's dissolution and liquidation, holders of preferred shares may receive a share of dividends before common stockholders.

Redemption -- Regardless of the share owners' objections, the corporation may be given the right to purchase preferred shares.

Conversion -- The corporation may convert preferred shares to common shares, assuming this is stated in the articles of incorporation.

Voting rights -- Unless otherwise stated in the articles of incorporation, preferred shareholders generally have no voting rights.

Par shares -- Shares possess a specific dollar amount, determined by the board and specified in the articles of incorporation, which is indicated directly on the share certificate.

No-par shares -- shares issued for any amount assigned, whether arbitrarily or otherwise, by the board

Treasury shares -- shares issued and subsequently reissued by the corporation;; treasury shares may be reissued for less than their fair value, even if it is less than the stated or par value.

Discount shares -- shares issued for less than par value; the purchaser of such shares is liable to the corporation for the amount of the discount.

Practice Test

Want to take this practice test in an online interactive format?
Check out the online resources page, which includes interactive practice questions and much more: **mometrix.com/resources719/clepintrobusl**

1. A customer at Giordano's grocery store spills some soda on the floor. Two hours later, Brent slips on the spill and throws out his back. Which of the following best describes Brent's legal options?

a. He can recover damages from the person who spilled the soda.
b. He can recover damages from the grocery store if the floors have not been checked regularly and well.
c. He cannot recover damages from the grocery store if the floors are cleaned every day.
d. He cannot recover damages from the grocery store if employees did not know about the spill.
e. He has no legal recourse.

2. What is the name for unintentional but materially false statements made by one party, which can be used to justify rescission of a contract?

a. actual fraud
b. misrepresentation
c. interference with business relations
d. conspiracy
e. constructive fraud

3. Which of the following is NOT a necessary part of a contract?

a. legal capacity
b. offer and acceptance
c. legal objective
d. consideration
e. documentation

4. Which of the following is NOT a potential result of a civil proceeding?

a. imprisonment
b. temporary restraining order
c. compensatory damages
d. acquittal
e. declaratory relief

5. Which body or bodies regulate the ethics of the medical profession?

a. state medical associations
b. state legislatures
c. United States Surgeon General
d. federal administrative agencies
e. United States Congress

6. According to which theory of jurisprudence are laws based on transcendent principles rather than on tradition or social custom?

a. federalism
b. natural law
c. critical legalism
d. legal positivism
e. legal realism

7. Dean borrows Sally's computer without asking. While he has it in his possession, he drops it, causing minor damage to the keyboard. Which tort would include Dean's liability to Sally in this scenario?

a. conversion for the full value of the property
b. conversion for the actual damages
c. trespass to personal property for actual damages
d. transferred intent
e. trespass to personal property for the full value of the property

8. Which of the following is required for there to be consideration for a contract?

a. genuineness of assent
b. a promise of cash payments
c. a bargained-for disadvantage to the promisor(ee) or an advantage to the promisee(or)
d. substantially equal economic benefits to both parties
e. manifestation of mutual assent

9. Which of the following duties does a corporation owe to its workers?

a. positive work environment
b. high wages
c. smoking breaks
d. a competitive wage
e. A corporation owes no duties to its workers.

10. What is the name of the post-judgment remedy that allows a sheriff to seize and sell the nonexempt property of a debtor?

a. writ of execution
b. writ of certiorari
c. garnishment
d. sequestration
e. attachment

11. Which of the following best describes the effect of a breach of contract?

a. Nonmaterial breaches that are uncorrected for a reasonable time discharge the other party.
b. Any breach discharges the other party.
c. No breaches automatically discharge the other party.
d. If the breach is material and uncorrected, the other party is discharged.
e. Nonmaterial breaches do not enable action for damages.

12. Who is allowed to enter into a hot cargo contract?

a. unions and employers
b. employers and nonunionized employees
c. neither unions nor employers
d. unions, but not employers
e. unions, employers, and nonunionized employees

13. What does it mean to say that the American legal system is adversarial?

a. American citizens have the right to representation in court.
b. The court system should appoint attorneys to represent both sides of a case.
c. Truth and justice are best determined by an independent researcher.
d. The best way to administer justice is to hear the full arguments of interested parties on both sides.
e. People with a personal interest in a case make terrible advocates.

14. Which type of warranty assures the buyer that the goods will be up to his or her standard?

a. express warranty
b. warranty of title
c. implied warranty of merchantability
d. lifetime warranty
e. implied warranty of fitness for a particular purpose

15. Which of the following facts would void the contracts of a person?

a. The person suffers extreme hardship.
b. The person is under guardianship of a court.
c. The person has not been declared incompetent by a court but lacks the capacity to understand.
d. The person is intoxicated.
e. The person is a minor.

16. In which of the following scenarios would Tina be liable for the tort of negligence?

a. Tina suffers a heart attack while driving and slams into another car.
b. Tina dunks a basketball and, because of a structural defect, the backboard crashes down and injures her teammate.
c. Tina takes cold medication that warns of drowsiness as a possible side effect. She subsequently falls asleep while driving and injures another driver.
d. Tina breaks into her high school and alters her grades.
e. Tina tries to hit her professor with a rock, but misses and hits another student instead.

17. Which of the following is required for consideration to be valid in a contract?

a. Consideration must be stated in the contract.
b. Consideration must have a monetary value.
c. Consideration must be accompanied by an option.
d. Consideration must be performed simultaneously by both parties.
e. Consideration must be based on a legal obligation rather than a moral obligation.

18. Which sales are regulated by Article 2 of the Uniform Commercial Code?

a. copyright sales
b. real property sales
c. sales of services
d. trademark sales
e. sales of tangible personal property

19. Which power enables courts to evaluate laws and declare them unconstitutional?

a. stare decisis
b. equal protection
c. rational basis test
d. judicial review
e. intermediate scrutiny

20. Which economist asserted that corporations should obey laws and social customs, but otherwise should concentrate all of their resources on making a profit?

a. Adolph Berle
b. Milton Friedman
c. John Maynard Keynes
d. Adam Smith
e. A.B. Carroll

21. Which of the following statements about the Supreme Court is true?

a. The Supreme Court always requests a writ of certiorari.
b. The Supreme Court has no original jurisdiction.
c. The Supreme Court has no discretionary appellate jurisdiction.
d. The Supreme Court has mandatory appellate jurisdiction.
e. The Supreme Court sometimes acts like a trial court.

22. What is the name for the international business contract clause that asserts the application of a particular country's laws?

a. force majeure
b. choice of forum
c. attorney fees clause
d. non-waiver clause
e. choice of law

23. Dave's Auto Shop agrees to transfer its entire inventory of sparkplugs to Fireplugs, Inc. Both parties agree to conduct this transfer according to the Uniform Commercial Code Bulk Transfers Article. What must be included in the notice to creditors?

a. The name of the lending institution associated with Fireplugs, Inc.
b. Whether Dave's Auto Shop will be paying off its debts in full because of this transfer
c. The names and addresses of Dave's Auto Shop's creditors
d. The confirmation of a bulk transfer
e. The quantity of sparkplugs

24. Geoffrey is an attorney, and Kelly is one of his clients. Kelly is unable to repay her large debts, and some of her creditors are threatening to force her into bankruptcy. She does not want to enter bankruptcy. Which of the following statements is true?

a. Kelly can borrow the money to repay her debts.
b. Kelly may be able to avoid bankruptcy by agreeing with her creditors to form a creditor's committee.
c. Kelly cannot be forced into bankruptcy.
d. So long as a custodian has not taken control of her property, Kelly cannot be forced into bankruptcy.
e. Geoffrey and Kelly should prepare financial statements that indicate solvency, even if these statements violate the accepted principles of accounting.

25. Company A airs a television advertisement stating that the products made by Company B have a structural defect. Because of this, Company B loses a great deal of business. What theory of tort would Company B try to use in an action against Company A?

a. vicarious liability
b. interference with business relations
c. trade libel
d. deceit
e. transferred intent

26. What is the most common approach to environmental regulation in the United States?

a. charging businesses for pollution
b. establishing standards and applying penalties for noncompliance
c. establishing private markets in which pollution rights can be purchased and sold
d. leaving pollution regulation to the state governments
e. focusing on large polluters and ignoring lesser infractions

27. Which of the following is a true statement about the Statute of Frauds?

a. It mandates that the independent promise to pay the debt of another be in writing.
b. It applies to all real estate leases.
c. It forbids the use of oral evidence to contradict the terms of a written contract.
d. It applies to all contracts with consideration valued at $500 or more.
e. It mandates that executory promises be written.

28. Who may file a voluntary petition for bankruptcy?

a. all insolvent debtors
b. only businesses that want to continue operations
c. corporations that have attempted to reorganize and failed
d. most debtors, even those who are solvent
e. all debtors, so long as most of their creditors have not obtained a receivership

29. According to which ethical theory is the right action that which creates the most happiness for the most people?

a. legalism
b. egoism
c. naturalism
d. structuralism
e. utilitarianism

30. When does the mailbox rule NOT apply?

a. both the offeror and offeree are merchants
b. the offer states explicitly that acceptance is effective only when it is received
c. one of the parties lacks legal capacity
d. the offer involves a real estate transaction
e. the duration of the offer is no more than three months

31. What is the legal term for the interpretation of laws by the courts?

a. judicial review
b. adjudication
c. statutory construction
d. judicial legislation
e. stare decisis

32. Darren rents a moving van from ACE Movers, Inc. Despite obeying the traffic laws and wearing his seat belt, Darren wrecks the van when the brakes go out. Which of the following statements about a potential tort suit to prove strict liability on the part of ACE is true?

a. Darren does not need to prove that the brake problems resulted in his accident.
b. Darren must have been within ten miles of ACE Movers to collect damages.
c. Darren may be able to recover damages even though he never owned the van.
d. Darren is required to show that the moving van was inherently dangerous.
e. Darren could not win a tort suit.

33. Which of the following classifications of state law has the LEAST authority?

a. regulations
b. state constitution
c. uniform laws
d. statutes
e. common law

34. An American company wants to sell bread machines to a corporation in France, but is unsure that the French corporation will be able to pay. What should the American company do?

a. require the French corporation to obtain a letter of credit
b. assume that American law will require the French corporation to pay
c. hire an accountant to investigate the French corporation
d. assume that French law will require the French corporation to pay
e. decline to do business with the French corporation

35. On Thursday, Dennis agreed to provide a week of tennis lessons to Abner, to sell his car to Ben, and to borrow $1,000 from Carla. On Friday, Dennis dies. His estate does not fulfill any of his obligations. Who could the estate prevail against in an action?

a. Abner
b. Ben
c. Carla
d. Abner and Ben
e. The estate could not prevail in an action against Abner, Ben, or Carla.

36. Which of the following is least likely to count as a signature according to the Statute of Frauds?

a. initials
b. signature in red ink
c. printed form with stamped name of the company on the signature line
d. signature at the top of a memo
e. printed name on a letterhead

37. How do US antitrust laws apply to foreign commerce?

a. They do not apply.
b. They apply only to foreign commerce transacted in the United States.
c. They do not apply to commerce that takes place in other countries.
d. They may be applied whenever the United States government likes.
e. They apply only when foreign commerce has an effect on American commerce.

38. What is the name for the clause that declares that all of the agreements made by the various parties are contained within the given contract?

a. performance clause
b. hardship clause
c. entirety clause
d. integration clause
e. merger clause

39. Which term best describes the role of a director of a corporation?

a. principal
b. general
c. trustee
d. fiduciary
e. agent

40. Which of the following is NOT a valid basis for avoiding performance of a contract?

a. innocent misrepresentation
b. fraud
c. extreme hardship
d. severe intoxication at the time of agreement
e. mutual mistake of material fact

41. What is the name for the legal principle that makes previous decisions binding in new but similar cases?

a. judicial review
b. writ of certiorari
c. stare decisis
d. dictum
e. habeas corpus

42. Andrew sells some personal property to Belinda for $500. The payment is due thirty days after the date of delivery. Andrew then assigns the account to Neil without consideration. Which of the following actions would preclude revocation by Andrew?

a. notice to Neil by Andrew of revocation
b. death of Andrew
c. subsequent assignment of the same rights by Andrew to Melba
d. bankruptcy of Andrew
e. assignment by Neil to Dora for consideration

43. When is the acceptance of an offer for a bilateral contract effective under common law?

a. when it is expressed verbally
b. when it adds to or subtracts from the terms of the offer
c. when it is identical to the offer
d. when it is received by the offeree
e. when it elaborates on or otherwise alters a term of the offer

44. Which of the following remedies can be obtained from a criminal action?

a. declaratory judgments
b. punitive damages
c. fines
d. restitution
e. injunctions

45. What is the scope of the Sherman Act?

a. The Sherman Act applies to all unreasonable restraints of trade.
b. The Sherman Act applies to all restraints of trade.
c. The Sherman Act applies only to individuals acting on their own behalf.
d. The Sherman Act applies only to express agreements.
e. The Sherman Act applies only to corporate contracts.

46. Which contractual action does not require consideration in order to be effective and binding?

a. waiver of a breach
b. delegation of a contract
c. modification of a contract
d. composition with creditors
e. mutual rescission

47. Ivan decides to avoid buying stock in companies that operate in Country X, which has a poor human rights record. Which ethical issue does this scenario illustrate?

a. reverse discrimination
b. collectivism
c. social investing
d. constructive engagement
e. whistle blowing

48. Which of the following has the most legal authority in the United States?

a. United States Constitution
b. treaties signed by the United States government
c. statutes of the United States government
d. Uniform Commercial Code
e. United States regulations

49. Which of the following branches of law is considered public?

a. contract
b. property
c. family
d. tort
e. constitutional

50. If Fred decides to give Barbara power of attorney, which of the following statements correctly describes Barbara's authority?

a. It is viable only if Fred is an attorney.
b. It may be limited with regard to specific transactions.
c. It may extend beyond Fred's death.
d. It is viable only if an agreement is signed by both Fred and Barbara.
e. It is valid for all transactions.

51. Which of the following best describes the scope of the legal environment of business?

a. all of the interactions between law and business
b. includes regulation of business by the state, but does not include the effects on business of common law
c. includes only for-profit enterprise
d. consists of environmental laws regulating the effects of business
e. includes the effects of common law on business, but does not include regulation of business by the state

52. What is the result of right-to-work legislation?

a. It is illegal to force workers to join a union.
b. It is illegal to operate a nonunion shop.
c. It is legal to operate a closed shop.
d. Labor contracts must include minimum wage guarantees.
e. Labor contracts must include the deduction of union dues from wages.

53. Who may accept an offer?

a. only the designated offeree
b. only particular people named in the offer
c. the designated offeree and any assignee of the designated offeree
d. only the offeror
e. anyone who finds out about the offer before its acceptance by the designated offeree

54. Which of the following could apply to a person who violates the Clean Water Act?

a. civil liability for all harm caused by the violations
b. criminal liability, if the violations can be proved to be intentional
c. criminal and civil liability
d. criminal liability if the violations occurred on public land
e. no liability

55. What is another name for a contract that requires the employee to agree not to join a labor union?

a. whistle blowing
b. featherbedding
c. yellow-dog contract
d. closed shops
e. secondary boycott

56. Which of the following are the directors of a corporation NOT liable for?

a. diversion of corporate opportunities to themselves
b. lack of reasonable care
c. honest mistakes
d. insider trading
e. declaration of a dividend that is known by the director to impair legal capital

57. Which of the following is required to establish a relationship between a principal and an agent?

a. power of attorney
b. nonfinancial consideration
c. written agreement
d. meeting and consent to act
e. specified consideration

58. Hector discovers a large beetle baked into his microwavable chicken pot pie. Which theory of liability would be most appropriate for him to use?

a. res ipsa loquitor
b. assumption of the risk
c. strict liability for design defects
d. respondeat superior
e. prima facie

59. Yostal Corporation plans to do business in New Jersey, though it was incorporated in Delaware. All of the shareholders of Yostal Corporation live in New York. How would this corporation be described in New Jersey?

a. multinational corporation
b. foreign corporation
c. S corporation
d. domestic corporation
e. alien corporation

60. Which of the following is NOT required in an agency relationship?

a. agent is subject to the control of the principal
b. consideration
c. agent is a fiduciary in respect to the principal
d. creation by contract
e. agent acts on behalf of another party than him or herself

61. What is the most likely reason for a corporation to select S corporation status?

a. It needs to issue preferred stock.
b. It expects to lose money early on.
c. Shareholders want to eliminate personal liability for losses.
d. It wants to go public.
e. A creditor is asking the shareholders to take personal liability for inventory to be sold to the corporation.

62. How does the Clean Air Act define a major stationary source of air pollution?

a. any facility that emits air pollutants
b. any facility that emits one thousand or more tons of sulfur dioxide annually
c. any facility that emits twenty or more tons of any air pollutant annually
d. any facility that emits one hundred or more tons of any air pollutant annually
e. any facility that emits one hundred or more tons of sulfur dioxide annually

63. Perry's Plastics has a contract to supply Sherman's Shoes with all of the plastic to make special running shoes. One of Sherman's Shoes' competitors, Phil's Footwear, intentionally causes one of Perry's Plastics' subcontractors to delay delivery of material necessary for the creation of the plastic. This in turn causes a delay in the delivery of plastic to Sherman's Shoes, which costs Sherman's Shoes thousands of dollars. Which theory would Sherman's Shoes invoke to win an action against Phil's Footwear?

a. fraud
b. comparative negligence
c. breach of contract
d. interference with business relations
e. no action is possible

64. If Oregon issues a statute that commercial fishing off its coast is limited to state residents, and the United States government issues a statute that allows other commercial enterprises to fish there, what will be the result?

a. Oregon's statute will be struck down by the supremacy clause of the US Constitution.
b. Oregon's statute will be upheld by the police power of the states.
c. Oregon's statute will be struck down by the commerce clause of the US Constitution.
d. The statutes will cancel each other out.
e. Oregon's statute will be validated by federalism.

65. Jerry signs a contract to build a house. In the contract, he agrees to pay a certain amount for every day of construction after the agreed-upon date of completion. How are these daily payments categorized?

a. actual damages
b. liquidated damages
c. punitive damages
d. personal damages
e. compensatory damages

66. Which of the following is NOT within the powers of the Securities and Exchange Commission?

a. obtaining an injunction to stop trading of a particular security
b. suspending brokers and dealers
c. reviewing the purchase and sale of securities
d. suing for treble damages
e. initiating criminal proceedings against an accountant

67. Henry is a partner of Green, Davis, and Isaacson. He wants to sell or pledge all or part of his interest in the partnership. There is nothing related to this scenario in the partnership agreement. What are Henry's options?

a. He can sell or pledge his entire partnership interest without dissolving the partnership.
b. He can pledge his partnership interest if he has the consent of the other partners.
c. He cannot sell all of his partnership interest, but he can sell a part.
d. He cannot sell any of his interest without dissolving the partnership.
e. He can sell his entire partnership interest as well as his status as a partner.

68. Discount Shoes has a contest in which the customer who can correctly guess the number of pickled eggs in an enormous jar will win a free pair of shoes. Why is this NOT an illegal lottery?

a. It does not cross over state lines.
b. Customers are not forced to guess the number of pickled eggs.
c. There is no element of chance.
d. There is no consideration.
e. Lotteries are not illegal.

69. How definite and complete must an offer be in order to be effective?

a. absolutely definite and complete
b. neither definite nor complete
c. reasonably definite and complete
d. explicitly definite and complete with relation to all terms
e. somewhat definite and complete

70. What is the name of the constitutional right of states to protect the general welfare of their citizens?

a. habeas corpus
b. state police power
c. eminent domain
d. supremacy clause
e. sovereignty

71. Which of the following statements about torts is true?

a. A tort is a crime against the state.
b. The basis of a tort is behavior that is ruled to be socially unreasonable.
c. A tort is the same thing as a crime.
d. A tort is any breach of a contract.
e. In a tort suit, the burden of proof is on the defendant.

72. Assuming there is no specific provision otherwise, how are the losses of a general partnership allocated?

a. the same way as partnership profits
b. in proportion to the capital contributions of the partners
c. equally among the shareholders
d. equally among the partners
e. in proportion to the capital contributions and outstanding loan balances of the partners

73. Which of the following items is not subject to assignment?

a. construction contract
b. contract to perform certain services
c. compensation from an as-yet unsigned contract
d. contract to sell special goods
e. unearned salary

74. Which of the following is required for a tort of defamation?

a. composition of a text
b. willful communication of a falsehood
c. communication to a third party
d. proof of special damages
e. accusation of a crime of moral turpitude

75. Which of the following does NOT legally terminate an offer?

a. The offering party dies.
b. The recipient of the offer is declared insane.
c. The subject matter is damaged or destroyed.
d. The subject matter is sold to a third party.
e. An agreed-upon interval for acceptance expires.

76. Which of the following pricing agreements between competitors is legal?

a. an agreement to lower prices
b. an agreement to raise prices
c. an agreement to fix prices at a level beneficial to consumers
d. an agreement to stabilize prices in order to reduce competition
e. There are no legal pricing agreements between competitors.

77. In its annual report, Hendrix Corporation mentions that it is party to the lawsuit *Dealbusters, Inc. v. Tully Manufacturing*. What can be inferred from this?

a. The liability of Hendrix Corporation is very small.
b. The case is a criminal proceeding.
c. The plaintiff is Tully Manufacturing.
d. The plaintiff is Dealbusters, Inc.
e. The case is a civil proceeding.

78. What is another name for a contract implied in law?

a. implied contract
b. promise
c. pseudo-contract
d. express contract
e. quasi-contract

79. Which of the following is required for a tort of battery?

a. offensive or harmful contact to the body
b. the plaintiff's knowledge of the conduct of the defendant
c. the risk of harm to the defendant's body
d. a demonstration of damages by the plaintiff
e. intent by the defendant to cause battery

80. In which scenario is an adhesion contract most appropriate?

a. The contract will reduce transaction costs to the seller.
b. The buyer has much less bargaining power than the seller.
c. The seller makes only a few transactions.
d. The buyer wants to negotiate with the seller.
e. The seller refuses to negotiate with buyers and will sign only a standard contract with very favorable terms for the seller.

81. Which of the following does NOT dissolve a partnership?

a. bankruptcy of one partner, assuming other partners remain solvent
b. one partner's assignment of his or her entire partnership interest
c. voluntary withdrawal of one of the partners
d. death of a partner, so long as his or her will names a new partner
e. wrongful withdrawal by one partner in contravention of the partnership agreement

82. What is the legal name for a contract in which one party must complete all of its promises before the other begins?

a. divisible contract
b. executed contract
c. entire contract
d. implied contract
e. formal contract

83. Sparkington, Inc. manufactures and sells shoelaces. It has three competitors in the United States. Sparkington sells approximately 95% of the shoelaces sold in Florida, but only 15% of the shoelaces sold nationally. Which of the following scenarios is possible?

a. Sparkington could be found guilty of monopolization in any product market, because it has so few competitors.
b. Sparkington could not be found guilty of monopolization regardless of intent.
c. Sparkington could be found guilty of monopolization if the relevant product market is determined to be Florida.
d. Sparkington could not be found guilty of monopolization if it has not shown intent to monopolize.
e. Sparkington could be found guilty of monopolization in Florida if its competitors left this state due to a lack of total sales.

84. Brian is hired by Dumbo, Ltd. to work as a salesman for one year in exchange for $35,000 and 1.5% of sales. Which of the following statements is true?

a. The agreement between Brian and Dumbo is not enforceable unless it is in writing and signed by both parties.
b. Dumbo cannot fire Brian without cause during this year.
c. For the year of his employment, Brian is required to act in Dumbo's interest in all matters related to their business.
d. Brian will not make less than $40,000 in the coming year.
e. Brian cannot quit during this year.

85. Which body has the power to regulate bankruptcies?

a. Congress
b. federal government
c. Securities and Exchange Commission
d. state governments
e. Supreme Court

86. Paul is accused of a tort of defamation. Which of the following defenses could he use?

a. Even though Paul's statement was malicious, it was true.
b. Paul has a conditional privilege because he was called as a witness to testify in a suit to which the plaintiff in the defamation class was not a party.
c. The plaintiff's negligence has also contributed to his own harm.
d. Paul has an absolute privilege because he was a former employer asked to comment about the plaintiff, who was applying for another job.
e. Paul has a constitutional privilege as a public figure.

87. Which of the following is an example of moral hazard?

a. The government doesn't offer assistance to a failing bank.
b. Denise wrecks her car in front of three witnesses, and lies to the police officer about the accident.
c. Senator Blackwell doesn't report a campaign donation, even though he is required by law to do so.
d. Sloan steals fifty pens from her office supply closet.
e. Dave takes out a large insurance policy on his office, and is subsequently less interested in waterproofing it.

88. Which of the following must the plaintiff prove in a tort of negligence?

a. The defendant's conduct did not breach his or her duty.
b. The defendant intended to harm the plaintiff.
c. The action of the defendant was a proximate cause of the injury to the plaintiff.
d. The plaintiff owed a duty to the defendant.
e. The action taken by the defendant was abnormally dangerous.

89. Which of the following would still be legally binding for all parties despite a lack of consideration?

a. an employment agreement established orally for a term of six months from the date of agreement
b. a promise to provide six months of piano lessons
c. a material modification made to the contract to buy and sell a piece of land and agreed upon by both parties
d. a promise to donate money to a non-profit, if the non-profit relied on this promise while making purchases
e. a merchant's irrevocable oral promise to keep an offer open for a month

90. Which of the following statements about small claims court is true?

a. Small claims courts do not have to follow the ordinary rules of civil procedure.
b. Small claims courts do not take appeals.
c. Small claims courts do not establish jurisdictional amounts.
d. Small claims courts handle only cases of corporate law.
e. Small claims courts do not allow lawyers.

91. The security guard at K & M Department Store reasonably believed that he saw Brenda put a bottle of perfume in her pocket. When she left the store without paying for the perfume, he ran after her yelling. He finally caught up to her, twisted her arm, and pinned her against a brick wall in the parking garage until the police could arrive. Even though Brenda stole the perfume, could she sue the store for false imprisonment?

a. No, but she could sue the store for intentional infliction of emotional distress.
b. Yes, because the security guard exercised unreasonable force and used an unreasonable method of detaining her.
c. No, because the security guard had a reasonable belief that she had stolen the perfume.
d. Yes, because the employee of a private store cannot detain someone in a public place.
e. No, because Brenda stole the perfume.

92. Which of the following is most important when a court interprets a contract?

a. contract language
b. trade usage
c. course of dealing
d. essential terms
e. course of performance

93. To what extent do antitrust laws apply to regulated industries?

a. Regulated industries are exempt to the extent determined by the regulatory agency.
b. Regulated industries are not expressly or completely exempt from antitrust laws.
c. Regulated industries are exempt to the extent determined by federal statutes and courts.
d. Antitrust laws apply to regulated industries to the same extent as to all other industries.
e. Antitrust laws never apply to regulated industries.

94. Which law forbids deceptive credit arrangements that exploit consumers?

a. Fair Credit Reporting Act
b. Truth in Lending Act
c. Taft-Hartley Act
d. Lanham Act
e. Equal Credit Opportunity Act

95. Greasy Pete's Diner has assets of $25,000 and liabilities of $75,000. The owner of Greasy Pete's decides to make an assignment for the benefit of creditors to fulfill some of his liabilities. What will be the effect?

a. All of the creditors who agree to this deal will receive pro-rata payments.
b. All of the creditors who agree to this deal will receive equal payments.
c. No creditors will receive payment.
d. All creditors will receive equal payments.
e. All creditors will receive pro-rata payments.

96. What is the legal designation for a contract that is not effective and has no recognition under the law?

a. invalid
b. valid
c. unenforceable
d. negated
e. void

97. In which scenario can a manufacturer NOT be held liable for negligence?

a. The negligence occurred in the design of the product.
b. The materials used to manufacture the product were substandard.
c. The manufacturer failed to warn users of a potential danger.
d. The product is used in an unforeseeable, improper manner.
e. The product was assembled incorrectly.

98. In which scenario would Nebraska be unable to secure personal jurisdiction over Marvin?

a. Marvin agrees to appear in court in Nebraska.
b. Marvin's permanent address is in Nebraska, though he is currently in Ohio.
c. Marvin neither lives nor works in Nebraska, but he has several business relationships with Nebraskans.
d. Marvin is in Nebraska, but lives and works in Oklahoma.
e. Marvin was born in Nebraska, but he now lives and works in Michigan.

99. What is the name for a mutual agreement to return to the status before a contract was formed?

a. accord and satisfaction
b. rescission
c. novation
d. revocation
e. release

100. Darryl is fired by his employer. He is a member of a union that had a collective bargaining agreement with the employer under which unresolved grievances concerning termination are sent to binding arbitration. If Darryl files a grievance and the arbitrator rules in his favor, how could this result be reviewed?

a. The ruling will be reviewed by a federal court.
b. The ruling will probably not be reviewed by a court.
c. The ruling will be reviewed in small claims court.
d. The ruling will be reviewed by the National Labor Relations Board.
e. The ruling will be reviewed by a state court.

Answers and Explanations

1. B: If the floors have not been checked regularly and well, Brent could recover damages from the store. The owner of a store has a duty to maintain reasonable levels of safety within the store. If this duty is not fulfilled, a visitor to the store who sustains injuries can recover damages from the store. The responsibility for maintaining the floors, then, lies with the business and not with the person who made the spill. Simply cleaning the floors every day does not guarantee sufficient safety, since with this program a spill could potentially sit on the floor all day. Also, it does not matter if the employees knew about this specific spill, since they are responsible anyway.

2. B: Misrepresentation is the name for unintentional but materially false statements made by one party, which can be used to justify rescission of a contract. In order to justify rescission, misrepresentations must have helped convince the other party to enter the contract. Actual fraud is willful false representation designed to convince another party to enter a contract. Constructive fraud, on the other hand, is disregard for the truth. It is essentially gross negligence that leads to misrepresentation. Interference with business relations is deliberate meddling in or hindering of another party's economic activity. Conspiracy is unlawful collaboration between two or more parties to accomplish either an illegal goal or a legal goal though illegal means.

3. E: Documentation is not a necessary part of a contract. Although some contracts cannot be enforced without a written agreement, in most cases documentation is unnecessary. There are four required elements to a contract: offer and acceptance, consideration, legal capacity, and a legal objective. Legal capacity is the requisite soundness of mind and authority to make legal decisions. In an offer and acceptance, one side promises to provide something to the other side, and the other side agrees to receive it. The legal objective or purpose of a contract is the effect of the arrangement that is desired by both parties. Consideration is something of value that is given in exchange for the offer. In order for a contract to be valid, both sides must receive something of value.

4. A: Imprisonment is not a potential result of a civil proceeding. A civil proceeding is initiated by a party that desires to enforce or protect private rights. A criminal proceeding, on the other hand, is initiated by the state to punish wrongdoing. A person convicted in a criminal trial may be imprisoned. A temporary restraining order forbids the defendant from taking a certain action until a trial can be held. Compensatory damages are issued when the plaintiff's rights or property have been damaged but can be restored. Acquittal is a potential result of a civil proceeding, insofar as the defendant may be found not guilty. Declaratory relief is an official statement of the rights and responsibilities of both parties in a civil proceeding; it is not necessarily accompanied by other remedy.

5. A: State medical associations regulate the ethics of the medical profession. The ethical codes for the medical and legal professions are somewhat different from those of other professions. Doctors and lawyers are governed by state professional associations, and their codes of ethics are enforceable. In most other lines of work, the code of ethics is voluntary and established by a business association. In addition, doctors and lawyers must be licensed in order to perform their duties, while participants in most other trades do not. All of the other answer choices are offices or bodies that may affect the professional lives of doctors but are not primarily responsible for regulating medical ethics.

6. B: The natural law theory of jurisprudence asserts that laws are based on transcendent principles rather than on tradition or social custom. In other words, proponents of natural law believe that there is an inherently correct system of justice, which can be obtained through the exercise of reason. Federalism is the division of power between a central national government and strong state and local governments. Critical legalism considers the law as a set of rules with the underlying intent of maintaining the power of the upper class. Legal positivists deny any link between morality and law. Instead, they assert that law is the result of social relationships. The school of jurisprudence known as legal realism asserts that the law is what the law does; that is, law has no abstract meaning other than how it is used in society.

7. C: In this scenario, Dean would be liable to Sally under the tort of trespass to personal property for actual damages. Trespass to personal property is unjustifiable damage to someone else's personal property. The recovered damages are typically commensurate to the injury or loss of the property. Conversion, on the other hand, is behavior that prevents the plaintiff from using his or her personal property. Conversion typically indicates a more serious infraction than trespass. Theft, unlawful detainment, and destruction of property are all acts of conversion. Since the damage to the keyboard was only minor, Dean would be susceptible only to a tort of trespass. Transferred intent is the tort principle in which a person who intends to injure someone else but instead injures a third person will be charged as if he or she intended to injure the third person.

8. C: In order for there to be consideration for a contract, there must be a bargained-for disadvantage to the promisor(ee) or an advantage to the promisee(or). Of course, many contracts include consideration for both parties. For instance, in a contract for the sale of widgets, both the seller and the buyer act as both promisor and promisee. Answer choices A and E are both required for a valid contract, but are not specifically related to consideration. Consideration may take a number of different forms, and is not limited to cash payments. Also, the equality of the consideration in a contract is not relevant. Unless the consideration arrangement in a contract is incredibly exploitative, it will be upheld by the courts.

9. D: A corporation owes its workers a competitive wage. Specifically, a corporation is ethically bound to pay its employees whatever the market will bear. In the United States, a corporation is not expected to sacrifice profits in order to maintain salaries. Answer choices A, B, and C are things that a corporation *may* provide, but are not considered duties. A corporation will strive to create a positive working environment, but it is not required to do so. Also, a corporation would like to provide high wages, but may not be able to do so without endangering profits. Most corporations allow smoking breaks, but they are not required to do so. Finally, answer choice E is incorrect insofar as a corporation has a duty to provide its employees with a competitive wage.

10. A: Writ of execution is the post-judgment remedy that allows a sheriff to seize and sell the nonexempt property of a debtor. If the debtor can satisfy the debt in time, he or she may prevent the sale of the property. Typically, the debtor's home and important personal possessions are exempt from a writ of execution. Garnishment is the process whereby money of the debtor that is held by some other party, as for instance the debtor's employer, is applied to his or her debts. Sequestration is the practice of keeping witnesses or jurors isolated during a trial so that they cannot be influenced unduly. Attachment is taking personal property in order to satisfy a debt ordered by the court.

11. D: If the breach of a contract is material and uncorrected, the other party is discharged. In other words, the other party does not have to perform its share of the contract. Also, the party that is charged with the material breach may be subject to fines or other remedies. A nonmaterial breach, on the other hand, may not obviate the need for the non-breaching party to perform. However, a nonmaterial breach can be the basis of an action for damages. Material breaches automatically discharge the other party.

12. C: Neither unions nor employers are allowed to enter into a hot cargo contract. In a hot cargo contract, an employer and a union agree that the employer will not handle the goods of a certain other employer that is in conflict with the union. These contracts are a way for the union to gain leverage over an antagonistic employer. Hot cargo contracts are considered secondary boycotts, and as such are illegal under the Taft-Hartley and Landrum-Griffin Acts.

13. D: To say that the American legal system is adversarial means that it believes justice is best served when interested parties on both sides of a disputed issue are given a chance to make full arguments. One of the reasons this system is successful is that it guarantees high motivation on both sides of a case. In other words, since both the plaintiff and the defendant want to prevail, they will in most circumstances present their best possible case and thereby elucidate the pertinent issues. Answer choice A is a true statement, but does not relate to the question. Answer choice B is incorrect, because the court system appoints attorneys only when one party is unable to obtain one themselves. Answer choices C and E are false statements.

14. C: An implied warranty of merchantability assures the buyer that the goods will be up to his or her standard. This warranty guarantees that the product will be what it is expected to be. An express warranty describes the criteria for acceptability for the goods. The express warranty also often contains a protocol for returning unacceptable goods. A warranty of title assures the buyer that the seller has the right to sell the goods in question. A lifetime warranty assures the buyer that he or she will have an acceptable version of the product so long as the product is on the market. If the buyer's copy of the product is damaged or destroyed, the lifetime warranty guarantees repair or replacement. An implied warranty of fitness for a particular purpose assures the buyer not only that the product will be sound, but also that it will be appropriate for the special purposes of the buyer. This warranty is distinct from the implied warranty of merchantability because it requires the product to have particular characteristics besides being of acceptable quality.

15. B: The contracts of a person will be void if he or she is under the guardianship of a court. A person is under the guardianship of a court when he or she has been adjudicated as an incompetent. When this happens, all of the person's legal capacity is evacuated, and all of the contracts he or she has entered into are rendered void. Extreme hardship is not a reason to void contracts; both parties should be aware of the risks before entering into a legal agreement. A person who lacks the capacity to understand will not have his or her contracts voided until he or she is declared incompetent by the court. Answer choices D and E are scenarios in which a person's contracts may be voidable, but in which the impetus for this action must come from the purpose. In other words, contracts are not automatically void because a person was intoxicated or a minor. The person must petition the court for this action.

16. C: If Tina took cold medication that came with a warning about drowsiness and subsequently fell asleep while driving, she could be held liable for negligence for an accident resulting in injury to another person. Negligence is the absence of reasonable and prudent amounts of care in a given situation. If the packaging indicates that the drug causes drowsiness, then Tina should know better than to drive. Tina would not be liable in tort for an accident that is a result of a heart attack, so long as that heart attack was not reasonably foreseeable. In the case of the basketball hoop, Tina would have no way of knowing about the structural defect and therefore could not be charged with negligence. Tina would be charged with breaking and entering for the high school incident. Finally, Tina would be liable for battery for hitting another student with a rock, even if she was intending to hit someone else.

17. E: In order to be valid in a contract, consideration has to be a legal obligation rather than a moral obligation. In other words, consideration must constitute something that one party *has* to do rather than something that it *ought* to do. It is not necessary for consideration to be stated explicitly in the contract; it may be implied. Likewise, it is not necessary for the consideration to have a monetary value, so long as it is of some legal benefit to the promisee and some legal detriment to the promisor. Consideration need not be accompanied by an option, though it sometimes is. Finally, many times consideration is conditional, which would make it impossible for it to be performed simultaneously by both parties.

18. E: Sales of tangible personal property are regulated by Article 2 of the Uniform Commercial Code. In other words, this part of the UCC regulates the sale of things that have a physical existence, like chairs, apples, or widgets. It does not regulate the sale of services, copyrights, trademarks, or other intangibles. Real property is held distinct from personal property, and is therefore not governed by Article 2 of the Uniform Commercial Code.

19. D: Judicial review is the power of the courts to evaluate laws and declare them unconstitutional. Stare decisis is the principle whereby decisions made in earlier cases are applied to cases with similar fact patterns. Equal protection is the guarantee in the Fourteenth Amendment to the Constitution that all people will be treated equally by the law. The rational basis test is the judicial process for determining whether legislation is arbitrary or has a clear and reasonable purpose. This process is part of judicial review, but is used only when a plaintiff argues that a certain statute is irrational. The judicial policy of intermediate scrutiny is part of the equal protection clause. It asserts that legislation and government action related to sex and illegitimacy (as for instance in inheritance issues) must be substantially tied to a governmental issue. Basically, intermediate scrutiny is meant to keep the government out of private lives unless intervention is necessary.

20. B: Milton Friedman asserted that corporations should obey laws and social customs, but otherwise should concentrate all of their resources on making a profit. Adolph Berle asserted that corporations are primarily beholden to their shareholders rather than the general public. Friedman slightly refined this approach by emphasizing that corporations should focus on promoting the interests of shareholders only within the bounds of the law and social customs. John Maynard Keynes asserted that corporations should be put to work for the government and the people, and that they should seek to improve the lives of all people. Adam Smith advanced a more general theory, that society is best served when all people follow their own interests. His philosophy is similar to that of Berle. Finally, A.B. Carroll goes beyond Friedman to assert that corporations must not only obey the laws and social customs, but also abide by all the ethical rules of a society. Carroll held corporations to a higher standard of conduct than did Friedman.

21. E: In some cases, the Supreme Court acts like a trial court. This happens only very rarely, and occurs most often in cases related to foreign officials or in which a state is one of the parties. The Supreme Court does not always request a writ of certiorari; it does so only when it wishes to review a case from a lower court and there is no appeal structure available. The original jurisdiction of the Supreme Court is identical to that of other, lower federal courts, but the Supreme Court almost never exercises its right to this jurisdiction. Instead, the cases that come before the Supreme Court do so at the discretion of the justices. This means that the Supreme Court has no mandatory appellate jurisdiction.

22. E: The international business contract clause that asserts the application of a particular country's laws is called choice of law. This choice is binding in arbitration and typically honored in court. A force majeure clause declares that both parties will be free of the contract in the event of some catastrophic, unforeseeable event out of their control (for instance, a flood, war, or strike). A choice of forum clause specifies where any necessary litigation will occur. An attorney fees clause specifies that if there is any litigation between the two parties involved in the contract, the loser will have to pay the legal fees of the winner. A non-waiver clause ensures that the terms of the contract can be upheld even if one of the parties consistently violates them and the other party accepts the violation for a time.

23. B: The notice to creditors must state whether Dave's Auto Shop will be paying off its debts in full because of this transfer. Since the notice to creditors must be posted in advance of the transfer, it would be incorrect to include the confirmation of the bulk transfer. The information in answer choices A, C, and E does not need to be included in a notice to creditors. If debts are to be paid in full, the notice to creditors needs to include an address for invoices to be sent. If the debts are not to be paid in full, the notice to creditors needs to include sufficient information so that creditors can inspect the inventory of sparkplugs before the sale if they so desire.

24. B: In this scenario, Kelly may be able to avoid involuntary bankruptcy by agreeing with her creditors to form a creditor's committee. If Kelly does this, however, the committee will have total control over her business operations. This would be a good option for Kelly if she wants to avoid damaging her reputation. It may not be possible for Kelly to borrow enough money to repay her debts. She technically can be forced into bankruptcy if she is unable to meet her obligations on time. Finally, it is illegal to create misleading accounting documents.

25. C: Company B would try to assert a tort of trade libel in an action against Company A. However, Company B could prevail only if it could show that Company A knowingly made false statements in the advertisement. In other words, if the product made by Company B actually does have a structural defect, the tort suit will fail. Vicarious liability is blame assigned to one party based on the actions of another party. Interference with business relations is the intentional hindering of a valid and enforceable contract. Deceit, otherwise known as fraud, is intentional misrepresentation designed to persuade another party to enter a contractual relationship. Transferred intent is the tort principle in which a person who intends to injure someone else but instead injures a third person will be charged as if he or she intended to injure the third person.

26. B: In the United States, the most common approach to environmental regulation is establishing standards and applying penalties for noncompliance. In a sense, answer choice A is correct, because fines are levied against polluters. However, the phrasing of the answer gives the impression that pollution is allowed. There are no private markets for purchasing pollution rights, though this idea has been mentioned as a possible way to regulate carbon emissions. Although state governments do issue their own legislation, they are not entirely responsible for pollution control. Finally, environmental regulators enforce the laws in every situation, not just with regard to the largest polluters.

27. A: The Statute of Frauds mandates that the independent promise to pay the debt of another be in writing. This is known as a secondary promise (a primary promise is the promise to pay one's own debt). Real estate leases are not required to be in writing if they are for less than one year. The prohibition against oral evidence to contradict the terms of a written contract is the parol evidence rule rather than the Statute of Frauds. The Statute of Frauds covers agreements of all dollar amounts. Finally, the Statute of Frauds mandates that some executory promises be written, but not all. The determination of whether a promise must be written has more to do with the content of the contract than with the degree to which it has been performed.

28. D: Most debtors, even solvent ones, may file a voluntary petition for bankruptcy. A voluntary bankruptcy is a request for the discharge of debts under the terms of Chapter 7 of the Bankruptcy

Code. Businesses that file for voluntary bankruptcy are not required to continue operations. A business does not need to have attempted reorganization in order to file for voluntary bankruptcy. The presence of receiverships would not forbid voluntary bankruptcy, since the relief offered by the bankruptcy court would put a hold on the receivership proceedings.

29. E: According to utilitarianism, the right action is that which creates the most happiness for the most people. This theory of ethics differs from some others in that it focuses almost entirely on the results of action, rather than on the motives or the action itself. Legalism is just the general assumption that societies should be governed by a set of laws. Egoism is an ethical philosophy in which the needs of the individual are paramount. Some ethical philosophers declare that capitalism is based on egoism, since in capitalism every person is striving for his or her own happiness and success. Naturalism is a philosophical system in which all human actions are derived from nature, rather than transcendent truth. Structuralism is a doctrine asserting that the general organization of a society is more predictive of morality than the qualities of individual citizens.

30. B: The mailbox rule does not apply when the offer states explicitly that acceptance is effective only when it is received. According to the mailbox rule, acceptance is effective once it has been transmitted in the same manner as it was received. The rule was so named because most contracts were sent through the mail, and therefore acceptance was considered effective as soon as it was placed in the mailbox. However, if the offeror stipulates a different moment for acceptance to become effective, this change can be binding. The mailbox rule exists in both common law and the Uniform Commercial Code, so it would not matter if both parties were merchants. The lack of legal capacity could invalidate the contract, but would have no effect on the mailbox rule itself. The mailbox rule applies to both personal property and realty. Finally, the duration of the offer has no effect on the mailbox rule.

31. C: Statutory construction is the legal term for the interpretation of laws by the courts. The point of statutory construction is to clarify any murky areas within the law. Often, legislation has unforeseen side effects that must be addressed through the judicial system. Judicial review is the authority of the court to evaluate and overturn legislation. It is different from statutory construction in that it entails either acceptance or rejection of a law, rather than clarification or elaboration. Adjudication is simply the rendering of a verdict. Judicial legislation is incorrect because it implies that law is made rather than interpreted by the judicial system. Stare decisis is the legal principle that previous decisions will be used to decide subsequent cases with similar fact patterns.

32. C: In this scenario, Darren may be able to recover damages even though he never owned the van. Darren would bring a product liability action against ACE Movers. He would allege that the company rented defective goods to him, goods that were a proximate cause of his injury. To be successful, he would have to prove that the moving van was unreasonably dangerous, that he did not cause the brakes to go out, and that the failure of the brakes was the proximate cause of his injury.

33. E: Of the given classifications of state law, common law has the least authority. Just as the United States Constitution is the foremost law of the entire country, the state constitutions are the most authoritative state laws. Regulations are laws developed by state administrative agencies; they are valid so long as they are not in violation of federal law or the state constitution. Uniform laws are created by a federal commission and sent to all of the state legislatures for passage. Statutes are any legislative enactments. A statute may be one legislative act or a series of legislative acts joined together. Common law, also known as case law, is set by the decisions made in earlier cases. The decisions that make up the common law must conform to the laws established in the constitution and statutes.

34. A: The American company should require the French corporation to obtain a letter of credit. A letter of credit is an agreement with a lending institution that the institution will pay the requisite money when the terms of the contract are fulfilled. In an international transaction like this, it would be common for a French bank to agree with an American bank to handle the payment if the French corporation should fail to pay or should reject the delivery. It would be a bad idea to assume that the French corporation will pay. Investigation before the sale and litigation after the sale are both more expensive than obtaining a letter of credit.

35. A: Dennis's estate could prevail against an action brought by Abner. Dennis promised Abner a service, which it will obviously now be impossible for him to perform. The agreement with Abner is therefore excused by the court. The estate is capable of making good on Dennis' agreements with Ben and Carla, however, and therefore could not prevail in an action demanding fulfillment.

36. E: A printed name on a letterhead is the least likely to be recognized as a signature under the Statute of Frauds. The Statute of Frauds mandates that certain contracts be put in writing. In addition, it requires that such contracts be accompanied by a clear signature. The Statute has a fairly broad definition of what constitutes a signature: any marking that can be interpreted as endorsement of the contract is likely to receive that interpretation. However, a letterhead is primarily used for identification, and does not necessarily indicate approval. For this reason, it is the least likely to count as a signature.

37. E: American antitrust laws apply to foreign commerce when it has an effect on American commerce. The authority of the federal government to regulate any activity that affects American commerce is granted by the commerce clause of the US Constitution. This means that US antitrust laws can apply to commerce that takes place in other countries, so long as it can be proven to have impact in the United States. This last caveat underscores that the federal government cannot apply antitrust legislation whenever it likes.

38. C: The entirety clause declares that all of the agreements made by the various parties are contained within the given contract. Any modifications to a contract with an entirety clause must be placed in writing and signed. The performance clause of a contract describes the responsibilities of each party. A hardship clause is put in place to guard against situations in which a decline in circumstances for one party will create an unfair imbalance in the contract. An integration clause asserts that the current version of the contract is the final, unalterable version. A merger clause indicates that the current agreement is composed of terms from a number of previous agreements, but that only the terms in the present contract are enforceable.

39. D: The director of a corporation is best described as a fiduciary. This means that the director must act at all times in the best interest of the corporation, rather than in his or her own best interest. Clearly, the director is not a principal, since he or she serves at the pleasure of the shareholders. A director can be described neither as a general nor as an agent, since both of these roles allow autonomous action and a director must function as part of a board. Finally, a director of a corporation cannot be described as a trustee since he or she does not have the legal title to the corporation.

40. C: Extreme hardship is not a valid basis for avoiding performance of a contract. When entering into a contract, each party should be aware that circumstance may make performance very difficult in the future. Problems in the future do not eliminate the obligation of fulfilling the contract.

Innocent misrepresentation, fraud, severe intoxication at the time of agreement, and mutual mistake of material fact can all be the basis for avoiding performance, however. Innocent misrepresentation and fraud occur when one party provides falsities that influence the other party to enter the contract. It is difficult to prove severe intoxication at the time of agreement, but it can be done. Mutual mistake of material fact occurs when both parties realize later that the terms on which the contract was conceived were erroneous, and that the contract should be voided.

41. C: Stare decisis is the legal principle that makes previous decisions binding in new but similar cases. The name of this principle is from the Latin meaning "stand by what is decided." Judicial review is the authority of the court to evaluate and overturn laws and lower court decisions. A writ of certiorari is a request by a higher court for a transcript of a trial in a lower court. Dictum is any text related to a decision that does not have a direct relation to the decision. Habeas corpus (in Latin, "you shall have the body") is the responsibility to present a reason for detaining a person. Oftentimes, a prisoner will request a writ of habeas corpus to make the authorities produce the evidence against him or her.

42. E: An assignment by Neil to Dora in exchange for consideration would preclude revocation by Andrew. It is not always necessary for an assignment to include consideration, but when it does not, there remains a possibility of revocation. An assignment without consideration is known as a gratuitous assignment. Such an assignment could be revoked by the death, bankruptcy, or incompetence of the assignor, or by the subsequent assignment of the same rights to someone else. If there is consideration, however, there can be no revocation of the assignment.

43. C: The acceptance of an offer for a bilateral contract is effective under common law when it is identical to the offer. Common law governs acceptance in all cases except those specifically treated by the Uniform Commercial Code. According to common law, the acceptance of a bilateral offer is invalid if it varies in any way from the original offer. Any acceptance to a non-identical offer is considered as a counteroffer and does not establish a contractual relationship. Answer choice A is incorrect because it fails to indicate the quality of the bilateral offer, and answer choice D is incorrect because it fails to indicate whether the bilateral offer will be accepted.

44. C: Fines are among the remedies that can be obtained from a criminal action. A declaratory judgment is made when the legal rights of the plaintiff are dubious. It entails the official iteration of the rights and responsibilities of both parties, but is not necessarily accompanied by other remedy. Punitive damages are extracted when the wrong done by the defendant is considered excessive or extreme. Restitution is the return of damages to the afflicted party, and is mandated in a situation where a simple restoration of the arrangement before the trial will satisfy the plaintiff. An injunction is a court order that forbids the defendant from doing something or orders the defendant to do something. A criminal trial would not end in an injunction, since it can be assumed that criminal behavior is already forbidden by the law.

45. A: The Sherman Act applies to all unreasonable restraints of trade. This act, which was established in 1890, prohibits monopolies, conspiracies, unlawful contracts, and other means of hindering competition. However, the act has been successful only in stopping those practices that the court deems unreasonable. Some restraints of trade cannot be stopped. The Sherman Act most often is applied to groups of people and companies rather than to individuals acting on their own behalf. Express agreements are covered by the Sherman Act, but so are tacit agreements. Finally, the Sherman Act is often applied to corporate contracts, but it can be applied to the contracts of other business types as well.

46. A: The waiver of a breach does not require consideration in order to be effective and binding. A waiver is an intentional relinquishment of a right. It can be offered after the fact without consideration, though if it is issued in advance, it must be accompanied by consideration unless it is exempt under the Uniform Commercial Code. Answer choices B, C, and E are all significant contractual changes that require consideration. Composition with creditors, on the other hand, by definition includes consideration of the mutual promises made by the creditors.

47. C: This scenario illustrates social investing. Increasingly, individuals and businesses are basing their investment decisions on moral and ethical rationales. Many businesses avoid investing in morally dubious companies and countries because they fear criticism from their shareholders and from the general public. Moreover, individual investors have gradually come to understand that they can influence powerful governments and corporations with their investment choices. Reverse discrimination is unfair conduct towards a member of a majority group; for instance, some whites believe that affirmative action constitutes reverse discrimination. Collectivism is the distribution of all profits equally among the people. Constructive engagement is the policy of negotiating and communicating with a hostile or unsavory regime, in the hopes of improving its behavior. Whistle blowing is when an employee tells the authorities about some illegal, unsafe, or unethical practice taking place in his or her business.

48. A: The United States Constitution is the foremost legal authority. Indeed, all of the other laws in the United States are made only with the authority granted by the Constitution. Answer choices B and C, federal statutes and treaties, are second in authority only to the Constitution. The Uniform Commercial Code is a set of laws, distinct from common law, that govern the sale and purchase of all types of goods. United States regulations are created by administrative agencies, and can be created only where authorized by the Constitution.

49. E: Constitutional law is considered public. A branch of law is defined as public when it relates to the operations of governing bodies. Because constitutional law centers on the responsibilities of and restrictions on government, it is considered public law. Contract, property, family, and tort law are all considered areas of private (civil) law because they have only to do with the interactions between private citizens and organizations.

50. B: When Fred gives power of attorney to Barbara, her authority may be limited with regard to specific transactions. There are a couple of types of power of attorney, one that gives unlimited power to the agent and one that restricts the agent's authority to particular transactions. Fred does not need to be an attorney in order to grant power of attorney to Barbara. Barbara's authority as an agent ends with Fred's death. The power of attorney agreement needs only to be signed by Fred in order to be valid. Finally, as stated above, the power may be limited with respect to specific transactions.

51. A: The legal environment of business includes all of the interactions between law and business. It includes all types of businesses, from labor unions to manufacturers to non-profits. It includes both common law and statutory law, and therefore includes the regulation of business by the state. It includes but is not limited to laws related to the natural environment.

52. A: Right-to-work legislation makes it illegal to force workers to join a union. This legislation is a response by the states to the Taft-Hartley Act of 1947, which permitted the existence of union shops, in which new employees were required to join the union. The Taft-Hartley Act asserted, however, that union membership could not be made a prerequisite for employment. In addition, the act granted states the right to draft legislation outlawing mandatory union membership. Many states have subsequently established right-to-work laws.

53. A: Only the designated offeree may accept an offer. The offeror has the right to designate as many or as few offerees as he or she likes, and only these people may legally accept the offer. It is possible for an offeror to designate the general public as the offeree, in which case anyone may legally accept the offer. Status as an offeree may not be assigned. Answer choice B is incorrect because the offeror may also designate groups of people and entities, like corporations, as offerees.

54. C: A person who violates the Clean Water Act could be charged with civil and criminal liability. Violators of the CWA are subject to fines, imprisonment, damages, civil penalties, and other sanctions. The violation does not have to be intentional to create liability; it can be the result of negligence. It does not matter whether the violations occurred on public or private land.

55. C: In a yellow-dog contract, the employee promises not to join a labor union. These contracts are illegal, and all states give employees the right to join a labor union and pursue collective bargaining. Whistle blowing is when an employee tells law enforcement officials or the press about illegal or unethical practices in his or her workplace. Featherbedding is the illegal union practice of forcing a business to slow down production or hire unnecessary workers in order to maintain high employment numbers. A closed shop is a business that employs only union members. Closed shops were outlawed by the Taft-Hartley Act of 1947. A secondary boycott is an attempt by labor to convince others to stop doing business with a particular firm because that firm does business with another firm that is the subject of a strike and/or a primary boycott.

56. C: The directors of a corporation are not liable for honest mistakes. Directors are considered to be fiduciaries to the corporation; that is, they are required to act in the best interest of the corporation at all times. This means that answer choices A, C, D, and E all represent behavior for which a director would be liable. Directors cannot be expected to be perfect, however, and therefore they are not held liable for mistakes that are attributable to honest errors in judgment.

57. D: A meeting and consent to act are required to establish a relationship between a principal and an agent. In other words, the principal and the agent have to get together and agree on the duties of the agent. Power of attorney is only one of the common agency relationships. These relationships do not require consideration, financial or otherwise. Furthermore, they do not have to be written down; many valid agency relationships are merely implied by the actions of the agent.

58. A: In this scenario, it would be most appropriate for Hector to use the liability theory of res ipsa loquitor (Latin for "the facts speak for themselves"). In this theory of tort, a party is held liable for negligence based on the mere fact of the accident happening. There is no need to prove an unreasonable dereliction of some duty. The assumption of risk is a defense that suggests the plaintiff took on responsibility for the accident before it occurred. It would not be valid in this case, since Hector would have had no way of knowing there could be a beetle in his pie. Strict liability for design defects would not be appropriate in this case, since the beetle would not have been present by design. Respondeat superior (Latin for "let the superior reply") is the assertion that an employer be held responsible for the offenses of its employees, when they are committed in the line of work. Prima facie (Latin for "at first glance") is a legal phrase for the first appearance of a case.

59. B: In New Jersey, the Yostal Corporation would be described as a foreign corporation. Indeed, Yostal would be considered a foreign corporation in every other state than its state of incorporation (Delaware). Yostal would not be considered a multinational corporation unless it had ownership in multiple countries. Yostal could be an S corporation, but this designation has nothing to do with its state of incorporation. Yostal will be considered a domestic corporation only in Delaware. If it had been incorporated in another country, it would be considered an alien corporation by the United States.

60. D: An agency relationship does not require creation by contract. Instead, it may be implied by the duties that the agent performs on behalf of the principal. Agency relationships may develop as the result of an emergency, or they may become tacit when one party claims agency for another and the other fails to contradict this statement. All of the other answer choices represent necessities for an agency relationship.

61. B: The most likely reason for a corporation to select S corporation status is because it expects to lose money early on. The unique feature of an S corporation is that profits and losses flow through to the shareholders. This can be useful when a business is not expected to do well at first, because the shareholders can reap some tax advantages. S corporations cannot issue preferred stock. Also, since an S corporation can have no more than 35 shareholders, its stock could never be available to the general public. Finally, even though the profits and losses of an S corporation flow through to the shareholders, the shareholders do not become liable for the debts of the corporation.

62. D: The Clean Air Act defines a major stationary source of air pollution as any facility that emits one hundred or more tons of any air pollutant annually. Sulfur dioxide is one of six air pollutants listed, along with nitrogen oxides, particulates, hydrocarbons, carbon monoxide, and photochemical oxidants. Moreover, the CAA does not make a distinction between facilities that can produce over one hundred tons of air pollution annually and those that do; both are considered to be major stationary sources of air pollution.

63. D: Sherman's Shoes would use the theory of interference with business relations to win an action against Phil's Footwear. Interference with business relations is the intentional hindering of a valid and enforceable contract. It must be shown that the intentional actions of Phil's Footwear were a proximate cause of damages to Sherman's Shoes. Fraud is any deceptive or intentionally misleading representation of a factual matter. Comparative negligence exists when multiple parties fail to exercise reasonable amounts of care, resulting in damages to another party. In torts of comparative negligence, blame is parceled out on a percentage basis. Breach of contract is any action that violates the terms of the contract or otherwise makes performance impossible. A breach of contract is subject to remediation.

64. A: In this scenario, the supremacy clause of the US Constitution will strike down Oregon's statute. The United States Constitution is the foremost legal authority. Any laws made pursuant to its power are more powerful than laws created by the states. For this reason, the federal statute will overrule Oregon's statute despite the state's police power and the principle of federalism. In addition, the commerce clause of the Constitution is not applicable in this case, since the federal legislation does nothing to impede interstate commerce. Finally, there are no scenarios in which conflicting statutes cancel one another out; rather, it is the task of the judicial system to determine which statute has more authority.

65. B: In this scenario, daily payments are categorized as liquidated damages. These damages are usually specified in the contract. In order to be valid, liquidated damages have to be appropriate to the amount of damage related to the house being incomplete. As long as the damages are reasonable, they are not considered punitive. These damages are not considered actual, since it is almost impossible to determine the precise amount of damages in such a scenario. Also, damages are not considered compensatory since they are written into the original contract.

66. D: The Securities and Exchange Commission (SEC) does not have the power to sue for treble damages. Treble damages are assessed only in antitrust cases, in which the SEC has no role. In fact, the SEC does not have the power to obtain damages of any kind. The SEC does have the power to stop particular trades with an injunction, as well as to suspend the activities of specific brokers and dealers. The primary task of the SEC is to review the purchase and sale of securities, and one of the common actions taken by the SEC is to begin criminal proceedings against accountants who have been making false statements or otherwise breaking the law.

67. A: Henry can sell or pledge his entire partnership interest without dissolving the partnership. Only Henry's death, bankruptcy, expulsion from the partnership, or voluntary withdrawal may trigger dissolution. He may assign all or part of his interest without any danger to the long-term survival of the partnership. He does not need the consent of the other partners, so long as the buyer of his interest has no rights other than to collect profits. In order to grant full status as a partner, however, he would need the consent of the other partners.

68. D: This is not an illegal lottery because there is no consideration. In other words, customers do not have to give something to Discount Shoes in order to have a shot at the prize. If Discount Shoes were selling tickets for the lottery, however, it would be illegal. A lottery that crosses over state lines would be a violation of the Interstate Commerce Clause, but many lotteries that stay within the boundaries of one state are also illegal. Customers are not forced to guess the number of eggs, but neither do they have to provide any consideration, which would make the lottery illegal.

69. C: In order to be effective, an offer must be reasonably definite and complete. In other words, the terms of a contract will not be carried out if some crucial term is omitted, but otherwise will be enforceable. The judicial system tends to allow some flexibility with regard to wording so long as the meaning of the offer is clear. Some of the terms in the contract may be implied and the contract will remain valid. In some cases, the acceptance will be more definite than the offer. It is legal for the acceptance portion of the contract to fulfill the definiteness requirement.

70. B: State police power is the constitutional right of states to protect the general welfare of their citizens. Acts of state police power are considered legally valid unless they violate some federal statute. Habeas corpus is the responsibility to produce evidence against a detained person. Eminent domain is the authority of the government to condemn private property and convert it to public use. The supremacy clause of the US Constitution guarantees that federal legislation has more authority than state legislation. Sovereignty is the right of the state to enact whatever legislation it likes, so long as it does not conflict with federal legislation.

71. B: A tort must be based on socially unreasonable behavior. Basically, a tort is a private or civil injury or harmful action for which a remedy can be provided by the court. Behavior is considered unreasonable when the harm done to the personal or property rights of one party is greater than the gain obtained by the action of another party. Torts are not crimes against the state; they are damaging actions against other individuals. For this reason, torts are not considered to be the same thing as crimes. Some actions constitute both a tort and breach of contract, but in general the two categories are distinct. Finally, as in all cases, the burden of proof in a tort suit lies with the plaintiff.

72. A: So long as there is not a specific provision otherwise, the losses of a general partnership are allocated the same way as partnership profits. Answer choices B, D, and E all represent possible methods of allocation, but in order to be applicable; they must have been specified in the partnership agreement. Answer choice C is incorrect because partnerships do not have shareholders.

73. C: Compensation from an as-yet unsigned contract is not subject to assignment. Assignment is the transfer of real or personal property to another person. In most cases, the compensation from a contract is assignable. However, when the contract has not yet been signed, the assignor cannot be said to have ownership of the compensation, and therefore cannot assign it. Once the contract has been signed, the compensation is assignable. For instance, unearned salary (answer choice E) is assignable because the assignor has an agreement specifying that it will be paid.

74. C: Communication to a third party is required for a tort of defamation. Defamation is any speech, writing, or other communication that injures another person's reputation. This means that it does not require the composition of a text. Furthermore, it is not required for the communication to be intentional. The damages of defamation are presumed based on the nature of the communication, and therefore do not need to be proved. Accusing another person of a crime of moral turpitude is one of the forms of defamation, as indeed of slander or libel. However, there are other damaging statements that qualify as defamation.

75. D: An offer is not legally terminated when the subject matter is sold to a third party. In order for this sale to terminate the offer, the offeree must receive actual notice of the sale. At this point, the sale of the subject matter could be an appropriate basis for a revocation of the offer. If the offeree does not receive this notice, he or she may bind the offeror with a valid acceptance made after the sale. For this reason, it is important for the offeror to give actual notice of the sale as soon as possible. All of the answer choices describe situations that legally terminate an offer.

76. E: There are no legal pricing agreements between competitors. These sorts of agreements violate antitrust legislation. The agreements outlined in answer choices A, B, C, and D are all illegal because they would have the long-term effect of reducing or eliminating competition. Even an agreement to fix prices at a level beneficial to consumers could eventually compromise the economy, because fluctuations in other costs could make the fixed price untenable. For this reason, there is no such thing as a legal pricing agreement between competitors.

77. E: From the title of the lawsuit, it can be inferred that it is a civil proceeding. Criminal proceedings relate to violations of the laws of the state, and so the titles of these cases always begin with the name of the state (for example, *State of Kansas v. Donnelly*). The order of the names in a case does not necessarily indicate which side is the plaintiff and which the defendant. Also, the size of the liability cannot be inferred from the name of the case.

78. E: Another name for a contract implied in law is a quasi-contract. A quasi-contract is not based on any intention or expression by any party. Instead, quasi-contracts are created by the court system to prevent situations in which one party is exploited by another. Quasi-contracts become recognizable and therefore enforceable by law. Even though there is no exchange of promises in a quasi-contract, both parties can be held liable for any breaches.

79. A: A tort of battery requires offensive or harmful contact to the body. Battery is any wrongful physical violence. Assault is the threat of force, while battery is the actual use of it. These two torts are often linked. Battery can be proved even if the plaintiff is unaware of it at the time. It does not require proof of the risk of harm to the defendant's body. Furthermore, a tort of battery does not require the plaintiff to prove actual damages; an act may have resulted in no damages and yet still qualify as battery. Finally, the intentions of the defendant are not relevant in a case of battery.

80. A: An adhesion contract is particularly appropriate when such a contract will reduce transaction costs for the seller. Many large businesses enter into hundreds of small contracts, and the cost of negotiating all of these deals would be prohibitive if not for adhesion contracts. These contracts are typically used for inexpensive items and for small-scale arrangements. Courts will declare adhesion contracts unconscionable if they give the buyer little or no control over the terms of the contract.

81. B: One partner's assignment of his entire partnership interest does not dissolve the partnership. Indeed, a partner does not need to have the consent of the other partners in order to assign his or her interest, so long as the assignee only has the right to collect profits. Bankruptcy, voluntary withdrawal, death, and wrongful withdrawal can all dissolve a partnership. Bankruptcy and death automatically dissolve a partnership, while wrongful and voluntary withdrawals may lead to dissolution.

82. C: A contract in which one party must complete all of its promises before the other begins is called an entire contract or a whole contract. In other words, one party in such a contract cannot partially perform its duties and expect full performance by the other side. Indeed, failure to fulfill all of the promises of the contract constitutes a breach. In a divisible contract, on the other hand, partial performance by one party can necessitate partial performance by the other. In an executed contract, both sides have already performed all of their duties. An implied contract is formed not by the documented or explicit agreement of the parties, but is a necessary product of their relationship. A formal contract is sealed and placed on record with some authoritative body.

83. C: In this scenario, Sparkington could be found guilty of monopolization if the relevant product market is determined to be Florida. The determination of relevant product market is one of the most important steps in a monopoly case. A 95% share is generally considered to constitute monopoly, so if the relevant product market is defined as Florida, it is likely that Sparkington will be found guilty of monopolization. Sparkington's national market share is small enough that it could not be found guilty of monopolization if the relevant product market is the United States. A company can be found guilty of monopolization even if intent cannot be proven, so long as the monopoly is in part a result of predatory practices. However, Sparkington could not be found guilty of monopolization simply because competitors leave the market (answer choice E); predatory practice and/or intent to monopolize must be demonstrated.

84. C: Brian is required to act in the interest of Dumbo in all matters related to its business during the year of his employment. Brian has signed to act in a fiduciary relationship with Dumbo, which means he must serve their interests whenever possible. This agreement does not need to be in writing or signed by both parties in order to be enforceable. Dumbo has the right to fire Brian at any time over the next year, though the cause should be sufficient to avoid a wrongful termination suit. Brian's earnings could be less than $40,000, since he is only assured of making $35,000. Finally, Brian can quit during this year, though depending on the circumstances, Dumbo may seek some compensation for a breach of contract.

85. A: Congress has the power to regulate bankruptcies. This power is granted in Article I, Section 8 of the US Constitution. Answer choice B is too general to be correct. Answer choices C and E are factually incorrect. Answer choice D is incorrect because the Constitution explicitly states that the power to establish laws related to bankruptcies is granted to Congress, and that state laws must defer to federal laws on this matter.

86. A: To defend himself against a tort of defamation, Paul could claim that his statement was true even if it was malicious. Defamation is any speech, writing, or other communication that damages another person's reputation. Most of the time, communications are not considered to be defamatory if they are true. In rare cases, true statements are considered defamatory if they constitute an invasion of privacy. Witnesses in court are given an absolute rather than a conditional privilege. The negligence of the plaintiff would bear no relation to the communication made by Paul. The privilege to give honest comment about a potential hire is conditional rather than absolute, and it can be withdrawn when statements are dishonest and vicious. Finally, the constitutional privilege against defamation is meant to allow the general public to make negative statements about public figures so long as they are not knowingly dishonest or malicious.

87. E: Taking out a large insurance policy on a piece of real estate and subsequently losing interest in protecting it is an example of moral hazard. A moral hazard is a situation in which a party has less incentive to act morally. Because he knows that he will be compensated for flooding or water damage, Dave is less likely to waterproof the building. Insurance companies take this into account when issuing policies, and require policyholders to perform routine and necessary maintenance. The other scenarios fall short of moral hazard. For instance, if the government does not assist failing banks, then banks will be less likely to underperform and rely on the government. The presence of the witnesses should give Denise *less* incentive to lie about her accident. The campaign donation laws should *encourage* Senator Blackwell to report all contributions. Finally, there is nothing in answer choice D to suggest that the office arrangement encouraged Sloan to steal the pens.

88. C: In a tort of negligence, the plaintiff must prove that the action of the defendant was a proximate cause of the injury to the plaintiff. Negligence is the absence of reasonable and prudent amounts of care in a given situation. A tort of negligence requires the plaintiff to prove not only that the defendant breached his or her duty, but also that this breach was the proximate cause of the damages. Since negligence is not an intentional tort, the desire of the defendant to cause the damages is irrelevant. Likewise, it is immaterial whether the plaintiff owed a duty to the defendant. Finally, the action taken by the defendant need not have been abnormally dangerous; indeed, abnormally dangerous behavior usually creates strict liability, whereas negligence is more likely to be charged for failure to perform normal duties.

89. D: Despite a lack of consideration, a promise to donate money to a non-profit would be legally binding for all parties if the non-profit relied on this promise while making purchases. Promises made to charity organizations are one of the few arrangements that can be considered legally binding despite a lack of consideration. The non-profit would obtain remedy through the theory of primary estoppel. In order to do so, however, it would have to prove that the promise of a donation could reasonably have induced some purchases, and that enforcement of the promise is the only means of justifying the promise. All of the other answer choices are situations that are not legally binding without consideration.

90. A: Small claims courts do not have to follow the ordinary rules of civil procedure. These are state courts that settle disputes over small amounts of money. One of the ways that small claims courts reduce costs for litigants is by avoiding some of the ordinary formalities of the judicial system. Although it is rare, some states do allow appeals of decisions made in small claims courts. Answer choice C is incorrect, insofar as most small claims courts establish a minimum jurisdictional amount (for instance, $1,000). Small claims courts rarely handle corporate law cases, and they do allow lawyers, though it is typical for both parties to represent themselves.

91. B: Brenda could sue the store for false imprisonment because the guard exercised unreasonable force and used an unreasonable method of detaining her. Store employees and security guards are given some right to detain suspects, even though they technically are not law enforcement officials. However, if the method of detainment is excessively violent, the security guard can be liable for false imprisonment. Under these circumstances, Brenda could not sue for intentional infliction of emotional distress, since the guard's desire to detain her is within his rights. Even if she stole the perfume, however, the guard does not have the right to use excessive force in detaining her. The fact that the detainment occurred in a public place does not matter.

92. A: When a court interprets a contract, the most important factor is the words of both parties. This means that the court will focus primarily on the language used during the formation of the contract. This is considered the best way to determine what was intended on both sides. Answer choice D falls under the heading of contract language, but is only a part of the discourse that contributes to contract formation. Answer choices B, C, and E are other factors considered by the court when interpreting a contract. Trade usage is the connotation of contract language in the particular industry or market in which the contract was signed. The course of dealing is the history of interactions between the two parties. The course of performance is the history of fulfillment of contract terms by both parties.

93. B: Regulated industries are not expressly or completely exempt from antitrust laws. However, the judicial system makes allowances for the limitations on competition that have been placed on these industries. For the most part, regulated industries are unable to undermine competition. If a regulated industry should seek to do so, though, it will be subject to penalty like any other industry. Answer choice A is incorrect because exemptions are not granted by regulatory agencies. Answer choice C is incorrect because regulated industries are not subject to the same degree of antitrust enforcement as unregulated industries.

94. B: The Truth in Lending Act prevents credit providers from misleading consumers and drawing them into exploitative relationships. This act mandates that credit proposals be presented in comprehensible language. The Fair Credit Reporting Act regulates how personal credit ratings are communicated to other parties. The Taft-Hartley Act regulates monopolies and trusts. The Lanham Act prevents trademark infringement. The Equal Credit Opportunity Act prevents credit providers from discriminating on the basis of age, gender, ethnicity, or race.

95. E: In this scenario, all creditors will receive pro-rata payments. In other words, the creditors will receive payments in proportion to their share of Greasy Pete's overall debts. The payments are calculated by multiplying the amount available for payment by the liability to the specific creditor and then dividing by the total liability to all creditors. These payments will be administered by a trustee. It is not necessary for the creditors to agree to this transaction, so answer choices A and B are incorrect.

96. E: A contract that is not effective and has no recognition under the law is designated as void. There is no remedy for a void agreement, and neither party is required to fulfill its obligations. An invalid contract has not been created properly, so either side can breach it without remedy. A valid contract is effective and can be enforced by law. An unenforceable contract may have been constructed in a valid manner, yet may have some inaccuracy that makes it possible for one side to avoid performance. There is no such thing as a negated contract.

97. D: A manufacturer cannot be held liable for negligence if the product is used in an unforeseeable, improper manner. In general, manufacturers are held liable for negligence when they fail to use reasonable care in the design, manufacture, and packaging of a product, and this lack of care is a proximate cause of injury. Negligence in design, materials, and assembly all create liability on the part of the manufacturer. Similarly, a manufacturer is liable if it fails to warn the customer about a danger associated with normal use of the product if that danger might not be readily apparent to the user. However, the manufacturer cannot be held liable if the customer is injured while using the product in an improper, unforeseeable manner.

98. E: Even though Marvin was born in Nebraska, that state would be unable to obtain personal jurisdiction over him if he no longer lives or has any business connections there. A state can obtain personal jurisdiction over people who are physically in the state; who have a permanent residence in the state; who have substantial business relationships within the state; or who voluntarily appear in court in the state. Once personal jurisdiction has been established, and the defendant has failed to contest it, it cannot be challenged in the future.

99. B: Rescission is the mutual agreement to return to the status before a contract was formed. The rescission of a contract means that neither side is required to perform the duties agreed to within the contract. Accord and satisfaction is an arrangement in which one party agrees to accept a different consideration as fulfillment of the contract. Both sides must agree to this alternate consideration in order for the agreement to be official. A novation is a replacement agreement, oftentimes including a new party. The creation of a novation renders the old contract obsolete. A revocation is the negation or voiding of a prior offer or contractual action. It does not create a new agreement. A release is an agreement that one party will waive the right to pursue legal claims against the other.

100. B: In this scenario, the arbitrator's ruling will probably not be reviewed by a court. This is because the federal government and almost all state governments have created legislation that declares binding arbitration irrevocable. One of the reasons for this is to eliminate the cost and time associated with litigation. Similarly, the National Labor Relations Board typically respects the ruling of the arbitrator. Only in rare cases, as for instance if the arbitrator acts in bad faith or the case falls outside the collective bargaining agreement, will the ruling be reviewed.

How to Overcome Test Anxiety

Just the thought of taking a test is enough to make most people a little nervous. A test is an important event that can have a long-term impact on your future, so it's important to take it seriously and it's natural to feel anxious about performing well. But just because anxiety is normal, that doesn't mean that it's helpful in test taking, or that you should simply accept it as part of your life. Anxiety can have a variety of effects. These effects can be mild, like making you feel slightly nervous, or severe, like blocking your ability to focus or remember even a simple detail.

If you experience test anxiety—whether severe or mild—it's important to know how to beat it. To discover this, first you need to understand what causes test anxiety.

Causes of Test Anxiety

While we often think of anxiety as an uncontrollable emotional state, it can actually be caused by simple, practical things. One of the most common causes of test anxiety is that a person does not feel adequately prepared for their test. This feeling can be the result of many different issues such as poor study habits or lack of organization, but the most common culprit is time management. Starting to study too late, failing to organize your study time to cover all of the material, or being distracted while you study will mean that you're not well prepared for the test. This may lead to cramming the night before, which will cause you to be physically and mentally exhausted for the test. Poor time management also contributes to feelings of stress, fear, and hopelessness as you realize you are not well prepared but don't know what to do about it.

Other times, test anxiety is not related to your preparation for the test but comes from unresolved fear. This may be a past failure on a test, or poor performance on tests in general. It may come from comparing yourself to others who seem to be performing better or from the stress of living up to expectations. Anxiety may be driven by fears of the future—how failure on this test would affect your educational and career goals. These fears are often completely irrational, but they can still negatively impact your test performance.

Elements of Test Anxiety

As mentioned earlier, test anxiety is considered to be an emotional state, but it has physical and mental components as well. Sometimes you may not even realize that you are suffering from test anxiety until you notice the physical symptoms. These can include trembling hands, rapid heartbeat, sweating, nausea, and tense muscles. Extreme anxiety may lead to fainting or vomiting. Obviously, any of these symptoms can have a negative impact on testing. It is important to recognize them as soon as they begin to occur so that you can address the problem before it damages your performance.

The mental components of test anxiety include trouble focusing and inability to remember learned information. During a test, your mind is on high alert, which can help you recall information and stay focused for an extended period of time. However, anxiety interferes with your mind's natural processes, causing you to blank out, even on the questions you know well. The strain of testing during anxiety makes it difficult to stay focused, especially on a test that may take several hours. Extreme anxiety can take a huge mental toll, making it difficult not only to recall test information but even to understand the test questions or pull your thoughts together.

Effects of Test Anxiety

Test anxiety is like a disease—if left untreated, it will get progressively worse. Anxiety leads to poor performance, and this reinforces the feelings of fear and failure, which in turn lead to poor performances on subsequent tests. It can grow from a mild nervousness to a crippling condition. If allowed to progress, test anxiety can have a big impact on your schooling, and consequently on your future.

Test anxiety can spread to other parts of your life. Anxiety on tests can become anxiety in any stressful situation, and blanking on a test can turn into panicking in a job situation. But fortunately, you don't have to let anxiety rule your testing and determine your grades. There are a number of relatively simple steps you can take to move past anxiety and function normally on a test and in the rest of life.

Physical Steps for Beating Test Anxiety

While test anxiety is a serious problem, the good news is that it can be overcome. It doesn't have to control your ability to think and remember information. While it may take time, you can begin taking steps today to beat anxiety.

Just as your first hint that you may be struggling with anxiety comes from the physical symptoms, the first step to treating it is also physical. Rest is crucial for having a clear, strong mind. If you are tired, it is much easier to give in to anxiety. But if you establish good sleep habits, your body and mind will be ready to perform optimally, without the strain of exhaustion. Additionally, sleeping well helps you to retain information better, so you're more likely to recall the answers when you see the test questions.

Getting good sleep means more than going to bed on time. It's important to allow your brain time to relax. Take study breaks from time to time so it doesn't get overworked, and don't study right before bed. Take time to rest your mind before trying to rest your body, or you may find it difficult to fall asleep.

Along with sleep, other aspects of physical health are important in preparing for a test. Good nutrition is vital for good brain function. Sugary foods and drinks may give a burst of energy but this burst is followed by a crash, both physically and emotionally. Instead, fuel your body with protein and vitamin-rich foods.

Also, drink plenty of water. Dehydration can lead to headaches and exhaustion, especially if your brain is already under stress from the rigors of the test. Particularly if your test is a long one, drink water during the breaks. And if possible, take an energy-boosting snack to eat between sections.

Along with sleep and diet, a third important part of physical health is exercise. Maintaining a steady workout schedule is helpful, but even taking 5-minute study breaks to walk can help get your blood pumping faster and clear your head. Exercise also releases endorphins, which contribute to a positive feeling and can help combat test anxiety.

When you nurture your physical health, you are also contributing to your mental health. If your body is healthy, your mind is much more likely to be healthy as well. So take time to rest, nourish your body with healthy food and water, and get moving as much as possible. Taking these physical steps will make you stronger and more able to take the mental steps necessary to overcome test anxiety.

Mental Steps for Beating Test Anxiety

Working on the mental side of test anxiety can be more challenging, but as with the physical side, there are clear steps you can take to overcome it. As mentioned earlier, test anxiety often stems from lack of preparation, so the obvious solution is to prepare for the test. Effective studying may be the most important weapon you have for beating test anxiety, but you can and should employ several other mental tools to combat fear.

First, boost your confidence by reminding yourself of past success—tests or projects that you aced. If you're putting as much effort into preparing for this test as you did for those, there's no reason you should expect to fail here. Work hard to prepare; then trust your preparation.

Second, surround yourself with encouraging people. It can be helpful to find a study group, but be sure that the people you're around will encourage a positive attitude. If you spend time with others who are anxious or cynical, this will only contribute to your own anxiety. Look for others who are motivated to study hard from a desire to succeed, not from a fear of failure.

Third, reward yourself. A test is physically and mentally tiring, even without anxiety, and it can be helpful to have something to look forward to. Plan an activity following the test, regardless of the outcome, such as going to a movie or getting ice cream.

When you are taking the test, if you find yourself beginning to feel anxious, remind yourself that you know the material. Visualize successfully completing the test. Then take a few deep, relaxing breaths and return to it. Work through the questions carefully but with confidence, knowing that you are capable of succeeding.

Developing a healthy mental approach to test taking will also aid in other areas of life. Test anxiety affects more than just the actual test—it can be damaging to your mental health and even contribute to depression. It's important to beat test anxiety before it becomes a problem for more than testing.

Study Strategy

Being prepared for the test is necessary to combat anxiety, but what does being prepared look like? You may study for hours on end and still not feel prepared. What you need is a strategy for test prep. The next few pages outline our recommended steps to help you plan out and conquer the challenge of preparation.

Step 1: Scope Out the Test

Learn everything you can about the format (multiple choice, essay, etc.) and what will be on the test. Gather any study materials, course outlines, or sample exams that may be available. Not only will this help you to prepare, but knowing what to expect can help to alleviate test anxiety.

Step 2: Map Out the Material

Look through the textbook or study guide and make note of how many chapters or sections it has. Then divide these over the time you have. For example, if a book has 15 chapters and you have five days to study, you need to cover three chapters each day. Even better, if you have the time, leave an extra day at the end for overall review after you have gone through the material in depth.

If time is limited, you may need to prioritize the material. Look through it and make note of which sections you think you already have a good grasp on, and which need review. While you are studying, skim quickly through the familiar sections and take more time on the challenging parts.

Write out your plan so you don't get lost as you go. Having a written plan also helps you feel more in control of the study, so anxiety is less likely to arise from feeling overwhelmed at the amount to cover.

Step 3: Gather Your Tools

Decide what study method works best for you. Do you prefer to highlight in the book as you study and then go back over the highlighted portions? Or do you type out notes of the important information? Or is it helpful to make flashcards that you can carry with you? Assemble the pens, index cards, highlighters, post-it notes, and any other materials you may need so you won't be distracted by getting up to find things while you study.

If you're having a hard time retaining the information or organizing your notes, experiment with different methods. For example, try color-coding by subject with colored pens, highlighters, or post-it notes. If you learn better by hearing, try recording yourself reading your notes so you can listen while in the car, working out, or simply sitting at your desk. Ask a friend to quiz you from your flashcards, or try teaching someone the material to solidify it in your mind.

Step 4: Create Your Environment

It's important to avoid distractions while you study. This includes both the obvious distractions like visitors and the subtle distractions like an uncomfortable chair (or a too-comfortable couch that makes you want to fall asleep). Set up the best study environment possible: good lighting and a comfortable work area. If background music helps you focus, you may want to turn it on, but otherwise keep the room quiet. If you are using a computer to take notes, be sure you don't have any other windows open, especially applications like social media, games, or anything else that could distract you. Silence your phone and turn off notifications. Be sure to keep water close by so you stay hydrated while you study (but avoid unhealthy drinks and snacks).

Also, take into account the best time of day to study. Are you freshest first thing in the morning? Try to set aside some time then to work through the material. Is your mind clearer in the afternoon or evening? Schedule your study session then. Another method is to study at the same time of day that you will take the test, so that your brain gets used to working on the material at that time and will be ready to focus at test time.

Step 5: Study!

Once you have done all the study preparation, it's time to settle into the actual studying. Sit down, take a few moments to settle your mind so you can focus, and begin to follow your study plan. Don't give in to distractions or let yourself procrastinate. This is your time to prepare so you'll be ready to fearlessly approach the test. Make the most of the time and stay focused.

Of course, you don't want to burn out. If you study too long you may find that you're not retaining the information very well. Take regular study breaks. For example, taking five minutes out of every hour to walk briskly, breathing deeply and swinging your arms, can help your mind stay fresh.

As you get to the end of each chapter or section, it's a good idea to do a quick review. Remind yourself of what you learned and work on any difficult parts. When you feel that you've mastered the material, move on to the next part. At the end of your study session, briefly skim through your notes again.

But while review is helpful, cramming last minute is NOT. If at all possible, work ahead so that you won't need to fit all your study into the last day. Cramming overloads your brain with more information than it can process and retain, and your tired mind may struggle to recall even previously learned information when it is overwhelmed with last-minute study. Also, the urgent nature of cramming and the stress placed on your brain contribute to anxiety. You'll be more likely to go to the test feeling unprepared and having trouble thinking clearly.

So don't cram, and don't stay up late before the test, even just to review your notes at a leisurely pace. Your brain needs rest more than it needs to go over the information again. In fact, plan to finish your studies by noon or early afternoon the day before the test. Give your brain the rest of the day to relax or focus on other things, and get a good night's sleep. Then you will be fresh for the test and better able to recall what you've studied.

Step 6: Take a Practice Test

Many courses offer sample tests, either online or in the study materials. This is an excellent resource to check whether you have mastered the material, as well as to prepare for the test format and environment.

Check the test format ahead of time: the number of questions, the type (multiple choice, free response, etc.), and the time limit. Then create a plan for working through them. For example, if you have 30 minutes to take a 60-question test, your limit is 30 seconds per question. Spend less time on the questions you know well so that you can take more time on the difficult ones.

If you have time to take several practice tests, take the first one open book, with no time limit. Work through the questions at your own pace and make sure you fully understand them. Gradually work up to taking a test under test conditions: sit at a desk with all study materials put away and set a timer. Pace yourself to make sure you finish the test with time to spare and go back to check your answers if you have time.

After each test, check your answers. On the questions you missed, be sure you understand why you missed them. Did you misread the question (tests can use tricky wording)? Did you forget the information? Or was it something you hadn't learned? Go back and study any shaky areas that the practice tests reveal.

Taking these tests not only helps with your grade, but also aids in combating test anxiety. If you're already used to the test conditions, you're less likely to worry about it, and working through tests until you're scoring well gives you a confidence boost. Go through the practice tests until you feel comfortable, and then you can go into the test knowing that you're ready for it.

Test Tips

On test day, you should be confident, knowing that you've prepared well and are ready to answer the questions. But aside from preparation, there are several test day strategies you can employ to maximize your performance.

First, as stated before, get a good night's sleep the night before the test (and for several nights before that, if possible). Go into the test with a fresh, alert mind rather than staying up late to study.

Try not to change too much about your normal routine on the day of the test. It's important to eat a nutritious breakfast, but if you normally don't eat breakfast at all, consider eating just a protein bar. If you're a coffee drinker, go ahead and have your normal coffee. Just make sure you time it so that the caffeine doesn't wear off right in the middle of your test. Avoid sugary beverages, and drink enough water to stay hydrated but not so much that you need a restroom break 10 minutes into the test. If your test isn't first thing in the morning, consider going for a walk or doing a light workout before the test to get your blood flowing.

Allow yourself enough time to get ready, and leave for the test with plenty of time to spare so you won't have the anxiety of scrambling to arrive in time. Another reason to be early is to select a good seat. It's helpful to sit away from doors and windows, which can be distracting. Find a good seat, get out your supplies, and settle your mind before the test begins.

When the test begins, start by going over the instructions carefully, even if you already know what to expect. Make sure you avoid any careless mistakes by following the directions.

Then begin working through the questions, pacing yourself as you've practiced. If you're not sure on an answer, don't spend too much time on it, and don't let it shake your confidence. Either skip it and come back later, or eliminate as many wrong answers as possible and guess among the remaining ones. Don't dwell on these questions as you continue—put them out of your mind and focus on what lies ahead.

Be sure to read all of the answer choices, even if you're sure the first one is the right answer. Sometimes you'll find a better one if you keep reading. But don't second-guess yourself if you do immediately know the answer. Your gut instinct is usually right. Don't let test anxiety rob you of the information you know.

If you have time at the end of the test (and if the test format allows), go back and review your answers. Be cautious about changing any, since your first instinct tends to be correct, but make sure you didn't misread any of the questions or accidentally mark the wrong answer choice. Look over any you skipped and make an educated guess.

At the end, leave the test feeling confident. You've done your best, so don't waste time worrying about your performance or wishing you could change anything. Instead, celebrate the successful completion of this test. And finally, use this test to learn how to deal with anxiety even better next time.

Review Video: Test Anxiety
Visit mometrix.com/academy and enter code: 100340

Important Qualification

Not all anxiety is created equal. If your test anxiety is causing major issues in your life beyond the classroom or testing center, or if you are experiencing troubling physical symptoms related to your anxiety, it may be a sign of a serious physiological or psychological condition. If this sounds like your situation, we strongly encourage you to seek professional help.

Online Resources

Due to our efforts to try to keep this book to a manageable length, we've created a link that will give you access to all of your online resources:

mometrix.com/resources719/clepintrobusl

It's Your Moment, Let's Celebrate It!

Share your story @mometrixtestpreparation